Lay Baptism Invalid

F. J. 25

Contents:

1) Lay baptism invalid
2) Sacerdotal powers
3) Brett (T.)

Lay Baptifm Invalid:

OR,

An ESSAY

To prove that

Such Baptifm

Is Null and Void ;

When Admininifter'd in oppofition to

The Divine Right

OF THE

Apoftolical Succeffion.

Occafioned chiefly by the Anti-Epilcopal Ufurpations of cur *Fnglifh* Diffenting Teachers.

The Second Edition Corrected and Enlarged. with an Appendix

By a Lay Hand.

To which is prefix'd a Letter to the Author by the
Reveiend *Geo Hicket*, D.D

St John xx 21, 23 *A. my Father hath fent me , even fo
fend I you — Whofe ever Sins ye remit, they are remitted
unto them*

Heb v 4 *No Man takth this Honour to himfelf, but he that
is called of God, is as Aaron*

LONDON Printed for *J Baker*, at the *Black-Boy* in
Pater-Nofter-Row and J Col at the *Black-boy*, in *Fleet-
ftreet*, 1709

A LETTER to the,

AUTHOR

S I R,

THE deplorable State of Christianity in those Parts of it which have
reform'd from Popery in Doctrine, is
chiefly to be ascrib'd to the Contempt or
Neglect of the Divine Institutions relating
to the Constitution and Oeconomy of the
Church. This in particular hath brought
all the Disorder and Confusion in matters
of Religion, for which *England* is scandalous above all other Christian Countries,
having ever since the Great Rebellion,
abounded with Religious Sects and Facti-
ons, which owe their Original, more or
less, to the direful change and overthrow
of that Government, which Christ ordain'd
for his Church, and his Apostles left in it,
and which throughout all Ages was continued without Interruption in the Christian
World for 1500 Years, as that very form of
Church Government, which all Christians
thought was ordain'd to continue unto the
End of the World. There never was in all
that time any Church founded but in, and

a   with

with **Episcopacy** ; nor did ever any Sect of Men assume the Title of a Church, till they could get a pretended Bishop, from whom they had their Priests, and their Priests their Mission, till the time of the Reformation; nor did any Christian Priests, or People of an Episcopal Church, ever rise up against their *Bishops as such*, and reject the *whole Order*, but those of *Great Britain*, under the pretence of farther Reformation, by which they have brought such Confusions, and so expos'd Religion among us, that it is in a great measure lost, so that we may say, (as was long since said of *Justice* in the *Iron-Age* of the World) that she hath taken her flight from Earth to Heaven. Could any Church, or Father of the Catholick Church, in Antient Times, have imagin'd or believ'd without the Gift of Prophecy, that an Age would come, when the Presbyters of a National Church would take upon them to *depose* their *Bishops*, and teach the People that their *Order* was contrary to God's Word, or grievous and unnecessary to the Church! Could they have imagin'd, that in a flourishing Church, pure in Doctrine and Worship, consisting of Two Provinces an Assembly of several Presbyters should be held in *opposition* to their Bishops,

and

and their Lawful Sovereign Lord the External or Civil Bishop of his Church, by the command of Rebels in actual Arms against their King! Could they ever imagine, that in three famous National Churches reform'd after the **Antient** Pattern of Churches settled in the Primitive Times, and professing the same Holy Faith, a strong Party of Presbyters and People, should be so wicked, as by *Force* to depose the whole College of Bishops, and as much as they could, extirpate the whole Order as unlawful and needless, nay, as an Anti-Christian Constitution, and a Yoak which we nor our Fathers were able to bear! Yet Sir, I am one of those surviving Men who liv'd in those times, and saw all those things done, and the direful consequences, the first of which was the setting up a Government of the Church by Presbyters assuming Episcopal Authority, who with their Sect were call'd *Presbyterians.*

But these did not long flourish; for as they had taught the People that Episcopal Ordinations or Missions were not necessary, so others soon said the same of their Ordinations by *Presbyters,* asserting, that only Gifts, and the *Call* of Gifted Men by the Congregation was sufficient for the Ministry; and so from the Sect of *Presbytery*

sprang

sprang up that of the *Independents* among us, and from them again, others, who thought Gifts *alone* were a sufficient Call to the Ministry, and in this *abomination of desolation*, *Laymen* first invaded the Sacred Office of the Ministry among us.

When I was a Young School Boy in a little Village near *Helmsley* in *Yorkshire*; I saw a Man in Gray Cloths step up into the Pulpit on the Lord's Day, where after a long Prayer he preach'd to the People, as well as I can guess from what I now remember, after the manner of the *Fifth Monarchy Anabaptists*. Being afterwards removed to School at *North-Allerton*, I saw an Officer of *Cromwell*'s Army go up into the Pulpit, and there after a long Prayer, he made a long Sermon, of which, as I then understood little, so I remember nothing, but that he talk'd much of *Dead Ordinances*, and Gifts of the Spirit, and a *Carnal Ministry*, meaning no doubt the *Ministry of the Church*. By that time *Quakerism*, which began in *Westmoreland*, was much increas'd in that Place, where I often saw not only Men, but Women Preach both in the Fields, and in Houses without any other call, but their pretended Motions of the Spirit, when (you must, Sir, excuse my impertinence to tell you, that) a
School-

School Fellow older than my self by 3 or
4 Years, though of a Lower Form in the
School, who had been carefully bred up
in *Church Principles,* and like another *Timothy* inſtructed by his Parents from his
Childhood in the Scriptures, ſo baffled their
Speakers, by asking them *who ſent them
to Preach,* and urging the places of Scripture againſt them, which ſpeak of God the
Father's ſending our Saviour, and *His*
ſending the Apoſtles, and *They* others;
and by requiring of them a *Viſible* proof
of their pretended Call by the Spirit, that
they came not of a long time after to that
place, and as I remember, not till that
Boy, ſo *mighty in the Scriptures,* was taken
from the School.

Indeed Sir, the Neceſſity of an *Immediate,* or *Mediate* Call and *Miſſion from God* to
any *Divine Miniſtry,* is ſo plainly taught in
the Scriptures as appears by the * Margin,
that I have often wonder'd how any ſort of

---

* **The Miſſion of Moſes.** — *And the Lord ſaid* ——
Come now therefore, and I will **ſend** *thee unto* Pharaoh,
that thou mayeſt bring forth my People, &c. out of Egypt.
Exod. 3. 10. *Now therefore go, and I will be with thy
Mouth, and teach thee what thou ſhalt ſay.* Exod 4. 12.
He **ſent** Moſes *his Servant* Pſal. 105. 26.
The Miſſion of the Jewiſh Prieſts, *Take thou unto
thee* Aaron *thy Brother, and his Sons with him, from
among the Children of* Iſrael, *that He may Miniſter*

a 3   Chriſtians

Chriſtians, pretending to the Knowledge of them, ſhould take upon them the Miniſterial Office, without the Ordinary Regular Call from Man as God hath appoint-

---

unto me *in the Prieſt's Office, even* Aaron, Nadab, *and* Abihu, Eleazer, *and* Ithamar, Aaron's *Sons.* Exod. 28. 1. *And the Lord ſpake unto* Aaron, —— *Thou and thy Sons with thee ſhall keep your* Prieſts Office. —— I have given *you Prieſts Office unto you as a Service of* Gift, *and the* Stranger *that cometh nigh (i e. as a Prieſt) ſhall be put to Death* Numb. 18 1, 7. Uzziah the *King tranſgreſſed againſt the Lord his God, and went into the Temple of the Lord to burn Incenſe upon the Altar of Incenſe, and* Azariah *the Prieſt went in after him, and with him Fourſcore Prieſts of the Lord that were valiant Men: And they* withſtood Uzziah *the King, and ſaid unto him, it* appertaineth not *unto thee* Uzziah *to burn Incenſe unto the Lord, but to the Prieſts the Sons of* Aaron, *that are* Conſecrated *to burn Incenſe.* Go out of the Sanctuary *for thou haſt treſpaſſed, &c.* 2 Chron 26. 16, 17, 18. *For every High Prieſt taken* from among Men, *is Ordain'd for Men in things pertaining to God, that he may offer both Gifts and Sacrifices for Sin. And no Man taketh this Honour unto himſelf but he that is* called of God *as was* Aaron, Heb 5. 1, 3. Not to ſpend too much time in enumerating thoſe Texts which prove the Miſſion of the Prophets, I ſhall only recite ſome of thoſe which plainly evince.

The Miſſion of St John the Baptiſt, the Laſt of the Jewiſh Prophets, and Immediate Fore-runner of our Saviour. *There was a* Man ſent *from God, whoſe Name was* John —— He was ſent *to bear witneſs of that Light (i. e. of* Chriſt) —— *He that* ſent *me to Baptize, &c,* St. John 1. 6, 8, 33. Behold ! I ſend my Meſſenger (i. e. John the Baptiſt) *before thy Face, which ſhall prepare thy Way before thee,* St. Mark 1 2. & 11. 10.

The Miſſion of Chriſt, The Second Perſon of the Eternal Trinity. —— St. *John* the Baptiſt ſpeaking of

ed,

ed, or an extraordinary Call from God, without one of which, neither Chrift, nor the Holy Spirit, neither Angels nor Men, prefumed to act authoritatively in things pertaining to God.

Him fays —*He it is, who coming after me is Preferred before me,* St. John 1. 27, 30. And our Lord fpeaking of himfelf fays, *He that receiveth me receiveth Lim* (i. e. God the Father) *that* fent *me,* St. Matth. 10. 40. St. John 13. 20 —*And He that defpifeth me defpifeth him that* fent *me,* St Luke 10. 16. — *God* fent *not his Son into the World to condemn the World, but that the World through him might be Saved,* St. John 3. 17. —— *Jefus faith,* —— *my Meat is to do the Will of him that* fent *me,* St. John 4. 34. —*He that honoureth not the Son, honoureth not the Father which hath* fent *Lm* —*He that heareth my Word and believeth on him that* fent *me hath Everlafting Life.* — *I feek not mine own Will but the Will of the Father which hath* fent *me.* — *The Father hath* fent *me.* — *And the Father himfelf which hath* fent *me,* St. John 5. 23, 24, 30, 36, 37. —— *The Living Father hath* fent *me,* St. John 6. 57. *The Father that* fent *me,* St. John 8. 16, 18. — *Say ye of him* (i. e. of Chrift) *whom* the *Father hath Sanctified* (i. e. Confecrated or Set apart for the Office of the Meffias) *and* fent *into the World, &c.* St. John 10. 36. — *That they may believe that thou haft* fent *me,* St. John 11. 42. — *I have not fpoken of my felf, but the Father which* fent *me, he* gave me a Commandment *what I fhould fay, and what I fhould fpeak,* St. John 12. 49. — *And this is Life Eternal, that they might know thee, the only True God, and Jefus Chrift whom thou* haft fent. — *I have finifhed the Work which thou* gaveft *me to do. I came* out from *thee.* —— *Thou haft* fent *me into the World.* —— *Thou haft* fent *me,* St. John 17. 3, 8, 18, 25 —— *God* fent *his only Begotten Son into the World, that we might live through him.* —— *And* fent *his Son to be the propitiation for our Sins,* 1 St. John 4, 9, 10. —— *God* fent forth

a 4 But

But moſt eſpecially have I wonder'd, and ſtill do wonder, how Clergy-men, I mean, Presbyters who were *regularly ſent*, by Epiſcopal Ordination, according to the

his Son made of a Woman, &c. Galat. 4. 4. —— Thus we ſee that *Chriſt* **glorified not himſelf** *to be made an High Prieſt, but He that ſaid unto him, Thou art my Son,* Heb. 5. 5. —— *Wherefore let us* —— *Conſider the Apoſtle and High Prieſt of our Profeſſion Chriſt Jeſus, who was* **Faithful** *to him that* **appointed** *him,* Heb. 3. 1, 2.

The Miſſion of the Holy Spirit, the Third Perſon of the Eternal Trinity. *The Comforter which is the Holy Ghoſt, whom the* **Father will ſend** *in my Name,* St. John 14. 26. —— *When the Comforter is come whom* **I will ſend** *unto you from the Father, even the Spirit of Truth, who proceedeth from the Father,* &c. St. John 15. 26. —— *If I go not away the Comforter will not come unto you, but if I Depart* **I will ſend** *him unto you,* St. John 16. 7. —— *He ſhall not ſpeak* **of Himſelf**, *but whatſoever he ſhall hear that ſhall he ſpeak,* ver. 13. —— *He ſhall glorifie me, for he ſhall* **receive of mine** *and ſhall ſhew it unto you,* ver. 14. —— Accordingly, the Holy Ghoſt was ſent from Heaven on the Day of Pentecoſt, as St. Peter teſtified to the wondring Multitude, telling them, —— *This Jeſus* —— *being by the Right Hand of God exalted, and having received of the Father the Promiſe of the Holy Ghoſt, he hath* **ſhed forth** *this, which you now ſee and hear* (i. e. he hath **ſent forth the Holy Ghoſt** who has cauſed thoſe aſtoniſhing Wonders which you now ſee and hear.) Acts 2. 32, 33. —— And St. *Paul* tells the *Galatians, God hath* **ſent forth** *the Spirit of his Son* (i. e. *the Holy Ghoſt*) *into your Hearts,* Galat. 4. 6. —— And St. *Peter* reckons *the Holy Ghoſt* **ſent down** *from Heaven,* among thoſe *things* which *the Angels deſire to look into,* 1 St. Pet. 1. 12.

The Miſſion of Angels. —— They are all *Miniſtring Spirits* **ſent forth** *to Miniſter,* Heb. 1. 14. —— *The Angel* **Gabriel was ſent** *from God unto a City &c. to a Virgin*

Will

Will of our Lord, the Founder of his Church, and the *Unvariable* and *Universal Apostolical* practice of it for 1500 Years, I say, I still wonder, how such Presbyters

---

espoused to a Man whose Name was Joseph, ——*St.* Luke 1. 26. —— The same Angel appeared before unto *Zacharias* and told him, —*I am* Gabriel *that stand in the presence of God, and* **am sent** *to speak unto thee.* —ver. 19. Peter *said, Now I know of a Surety that the* **Lord hath sent** *his Angel, and hath deliver'd me out of the Hand of* Herod, *&c.* Acts 12. 11. —— *The Revelation of Jesus Christ which God gave unto him,* &c. **He sent** *and signified it by his Angel unto his Servant* John, Revelat. 1 1. —— *The Seven Spirits of God* **sent forth** *into all the Earth,* Revelat. 5. 6. —— *The Lord God* **sent** *his Angel to shew unto his Servants the things which must shortly be done,* Revelat 22. 6.

The Mission of the Apostles After the Twelve Apostles *are* nam'd, 'tis said, These *Twelve* Jesus **sent forth,** *and commanded them saying* —— *Preach* ——*freely ye have* **received** *freely give,* St. Matth. 10. 5, 7, 8. — *As my Father hath sent me even so* **send** *I you,* St. John 20. 21. —— *All power is given unto me in Heaven and in Earth.* **Go ye** *therefore and teach* (or rather Disciple) *all Nations, baptizing them* ——*teaching them* ———— *and lo* **I am with you always** *even unto the end of the World. Amen.* St. Mat. 28. 18, 19, 20. — And to supply the Place of *Judas Iscariot* one of the Twelve, the Apostles *prayed and said, thou Lord which knowest the Hearts of all Men, shew whether of these Two* (i. e. of Justus or Matthias) *thou hast* **chosen,** *that he may* **take** *part of this Ministry and Apostleship,* Acts 1. 24, 25. *And they gave for their Lots, and the Lot fell upon Matthias, and he was numbred with the Eleven Apostles,* ver. 26. — God hath **set** *some in the Church,* **first** *Apostles,* 1 Cor. 12. 28. —*Our* Lord said to *Ananias* concerning the Apostle St. *Paul,* —*He is a* **chosen** *Vessel unto me to bear my Name before the Gentiles, and Kings, and the Children of Israel,* Acts 9. 15.

could

could firſt preach againſt the Epiſcopal Order, and then proceed to pull down their own Biſhops, by whom they were Ordain'd, and then in oppoſition to the Holy

—— As they Miniſter'd to *the Lord and Faſled, the Holy Ghoſt ſaid,* **ſeperate** me *Barnabas* and *Saul* (i. e. *Paul*) for the Work *whereunto I have* **called them.** *And when they had faſted and prayed, and laid their Hands on them they ſent them away ;* ſo they being **ſent forth** *by the Holy Ghoſt departed,* &c. Acts 13. 2, 3, 4. Again, *the Lord* ſaid unto St. Paul, *Depart, for I will* **ſend** *thee far hence unto the Gentiles,* Acts 22. 21. —— And therefore he ſtiles himſelf *Paul* **called** *to be an Apoſtle of Jeſus Chriſt, through the Will of God,* I Cor. 1. 1. and ſays in another Place, —— *I am* **Ordained** *a Preacher, and an Apoſtle* —— *a Teacher of the Gentiles,* I Tim. 2. 7. —— *How ſhall they Preach except they* **be ſent,** Rom. 10. 15. —— *When He* (i. e. Chriſt) *aſcended up on High,* —— *He* **gave** *ſome Apoſtles,* i. e. he gave ſome the Power and Authority of being his Ambaſſadors, *Epheſ* 4. 11.——

The Miſſion of the Seventy Diſciples, and of the **Deacons.** *After theſe things the Lord* **appointed** *other Seventy alſo,and* **ſent** *them Two and Two before his Face,* St Luke 10. 1. —— *The Twelve* (i. e. **the** Apoſtles) *called the Multitude of the Diſciples unto them and ſaid,* —— *Look ye out among you Seven Men of Honeſt Report full of the Holy Ghoſt and Wſdom, whom* **We may appoint,** *over this Buſineſs,* (i. e. of taking care for the Poor) —— *And they choſe Stephen, &c. whom they* **ſet before the Apoſtles** *; and when* **they** *had prayed* **they laid their Hands** *on them,* Acts 6. 3, 5, 6.——

The Miſſion of the Apoſtles Succeſſors. —S. *Paul* and St. *Barnabas* **Ordained** *them* **Elders** *in every Church,* Acts 14. 23. —— *For this cauſe left I thee* (i. e. Titus) *in Crete that thou ſhouldeſt ſet in order the things that are wanting, and* **Ordain** *Elders in every City, as I* (i. e. St. *Paul*) *had* **appointed** *thee,* Tit. 1. 5. — *Stir up the* **Gift** *of God which is in thee* (i. e. Stir up that Epiſcopal Authority, and the Gifts annex'd thereto, where-

Apoſtolical

Apoſtolical Order and Character, and the perſons lawfully veſted with it, Sacrilegiouſly preſume, like *Colluthus*, to take upon them the Epiſcopal Office, and power in Ordaining and Sending of other pretended Presbyters into the Church, as they did in

---

with God has endow'd thee) **by the putting on of my** (*i. e.* St. Paul's) **Hands**, 2 *Tim* 1. 6 — *The Things that thou haſt heard of me* ——— *the same* **commit thou** *to Faithful Men, who ſhall be able to Teach others also,* 2 *Tim.* 2. 2. ——— **Lay Hands** *ſuddenly on no Man,* 1 *Tim* 5. 22. —— *The Seven Stars are the* **Angels** (*i. e.* the Biſhops, or ſupream Spiritual Governours) *of the Seven Churches,* Rev. 1. 20. — Of which St. *Polycarp,* Biſhop of *Smyrna* was one. Now that theſe Succeſſors of the Apoſtles, to whom the Power of Ordaining others into the Miniſtry was committed, were not mere *Presbyters* is evident from hence, that they had the *overſight of the Church of God,* 1 Pet. 5. 2 A Power to *receive an* **Accuſation** *against* (and therefore were each of them a **Judge** of) an Elder or Miniſter of a conſequently Inferiour Order, 1 *Tim* 5. 19. — It was alſo their Province to *Rebuke with* **all Authority,** *ſo is to let no Man deſpiſe them,* Tit. 2. 15 —*to reject,* i e. excommunicate, *a Man that is an Heretick after the Firſt and Second Admonition,* Tit. 3. 10. — *Without* **preferring** *one before another, doing nothing by* **Partiality,** 1 *Tim* 5. 21. — Hence the particular *Angel,* or Biſhop *of the Church in Pergamos,* was juſtly reproved for Tolerating *them that held the Doctrine of Balaam, and the Nicolaitans* in that Church, *Rev.* 2. 14, 15, 16. So alſo was the particular Angel or Biſhop of *Thyatira,* for **ſuffering** the falſe Propheteſs *Jezabel,* Rev. 2. 20. — And they could never have been thus juſtly cenſur'd, if they had not been veſted with the Powers and Authority above mention'd, and theſe Powers do vaſtly exceed all that can be duly claim'd by any mere *Presbyter,* or Body of *Presbyters* whatſoever. ———

all

all, or moſt parts of the Nation, after the Abolition of Epiſcopacy, and the Downfall of the National Church with it, in the times of which I ſpeak. Such Archſchiſmaticks as theſe were Mr. *Bowls* of *York*, Mr. *Batxer* of *Kiderminſter*, and Mr. *Hughes* of *Plymouth*, not to mention *SMECTYMNUUS*, [*Stephen Marſhal, Edmond Calamy, Thomas Young, Matthew Newcomb, William Spurſtow,*] of *London*, where I preſume pretended Presbyters were alſo Ordain'd, by mere *Presbyters* in thoſe ſad times of confuſion.

I was once at one of their pretended Ordinations, which I ſince found, was much after the French Form. Thus, and This, Sir, was the Original of the *Presbyterian Miſſion* in *England*, and it is againſt the Authority of the pretended Miniſters of this Miſſion, *who were never duly Authoriz'd,* and therefore cannot Adminiſter *truly Valid Baptiſm,* that you have written your excellent Book with great Strength, and perſpicuity, as well as Modeſty, and confirmed your Doctrine with your Practice.

Indeed, you have written it throughout with ſo much Modeſty and Caution, that in ſome places, it hath an Air *almoſt* of Diffidence and Miſtruſt, although you have ſaid nothing as to the Invalidity of their Adminiſtrations, but what our

beſt

beſt Divines have written before you. I beg leave to preſent you with what I find to this purpoſe, in the Firſt Volume of the Poſthumous Sermons of one of the greateſt of them, [*Biſhop Beveridge*] enentituled, *The Dignity, and Authority, and Office of the Prieſthood.* In the Third Sermon on this Text, *Therefore, ſeeing we have this Miniſtry as we have received mercy, we faint not,* at the 103. Page you'll find theſe Words, " *In the next Place we muſt obſerve,* " *that although the Prieſts, if any be preſent,* " *lay on their Hands alſo, yet it is expreſly or-* " *der'd, that the Biſhop ſhall ſay the Words,* " Receive ye the Holy Ghoſt, &c. *For,* " *if a mere Prieſt ſhould ſay them, or any one* " *but a* Biſhop, *the Ordination was reckon-* " ed 𝕹𝖚𝖑𝖑 𝖆𝖓𝖉 𝖂𝖔𝖎𝖉, with more to that purpoſe. So in his Sermon on *Acts* 13. 3. " *And when they had faſted, and prayed, and* " *laid their Hands on them, they ſent them* " *away,* you have theſe Words at p. 309. " *As the right Ordination of thoſe, who* " *Adminiſter the Means of Grace muſt needs* " *be acknowledged to be* (neceſſary). *for ſee-* " *ing we can have no Grace, nor* P *wer to* " *do Good, but what is delivered to as from* ' *God through our Lord and Saviour Jeſus* " *Chriſt, in the uſe of the means which he* " *hath eſtabliſh'd for that purpoſe, unleſs thoſe* " *means* be *rightly and duly* Adminiſtred, " they

" they loose their Force, and Energy, and
" so can never attain the end, wherefore
" they were established. *Neither is there*
" *any thing more* necessary *to establish the*
" *means of Grace, than that they who Ad-*
" *minister them be* rightly Ordained and
" Authorized to do it *according to the Insti-*
" *tution, and Command of him that did*
" *establish them.* For seeing they do not
" work naturally, *but only by* virtue of the
Institution, and Promise annex'd to it, *un-*
" *less that be duly observed, we have no*
" *ground to expect, that* the Promise should
" be performed, *nor by consequence that they*
" *should be effectual to the Purposes for which*
" *they are used.* So in his Sermon on this Text.
" *Now then we are Ambassadors for Christ,* &c.
" p. 386. *For that can be done only by the power*
" *of God, accompanying, and assisting his own*
" *Institution and Commission. Insomuch that*
" *if I did not think,* or rather was not fully
" assured, that I had such a Commission to
" be an Ambassadour for Christ, and to act
" in his Name, *I should never think it worth*
" *the while to Preach, or execute my Ministe-*
" *rial Office.* For I am sure all that I did
" would be Null and Void of it self, *accord-*
" *ing to God's ordinary way of working, and*
" *we have no ground to expect Miracles.* So in
another Place of that Sermon ; " *Any Man*
" *may*

" may read a *Sermon* or *make an oration to the*
" *People, but it is not that, which the Scrip-*
" *ture calls* Preaching the Word of God, *un-*
" *less he be* SENT *by God to do it.* For how
" can they Preach except they be sent. *Rom.*
" 10. 16. *A Butcher might kill an Ox, or a*
" *Lamb as well as the High-priest, but it was*
" no Sacrifice to God, unless a Priest did it.
" And *no Man taketh this Honour to himself,*
" *but he that is called of God,* as was *Aaron,*
&c. All these Passages, Sir, exactly agree
with the Subject of your Book, and I might
shew you much more to the same purpose
out of the Writings of the Clergy, besides
those, which you have cited, *p.* 101. as out of
the Second Edition of a Letter to a Noncon
Minister of the Kirk, shewing the Nullity of the
Presbyterian Mission. And Dr. *Wells's Theses*
against the Validity of Presbyterian Ordination.

But what I have cited from the Bishop,
which was Published since the First Edition
of your Book, is enough to second the design
of it, and give you courage boldly to maintain your Doctrine and Practise, and the
cause not only of the Church of *England,* but
of the Catholick Church against the *British*
Sects and Schisms. Indeed you have done
God and his Church good service in a time
of need, as Two worthy Citizens now
with God, Mr. *Allen,* and Mr. *Lamb* did
by their Writings about Forty Years ago,
who

who having gone from the Church to the *Anabaptifts*, by God's Grace faw their Errour, and returned both together from them to the Church again, to which they made ample recompence by their Writings, and were great Ornaments to it in every refpect all their Lives long. I knew them both very well, and am glad of this opportunity, to mention them with that refpect which is due to both their Memories, whereof the former told me, that he had the Misfortune to lead Mr. *Allen* out the of Church to the Schifm, but that Mr. *Allen* had the bleffed part to lead him out of the Schifm to the Church again. It is to me a comfortable prefage, that God will not forfake the Church of *England* nor fuffer Toleration, and the Gates of Hell to prevail againft her, becaufe he raifes out of her People, Men to defend her, and adorn her with their Writings. I pray God to ftir up more fuch continually, that thofe, who are mifled by unauthorized Minifters, and Teachers, may confider the great danger they are in, and after your Example, enter in at the right Door into her Fold, and declare, as you have bravely done, *p.* 119, 120. *that you fincerely believe the Subject of your Difcourfe to be a fubftantial Truth, nay even a firft Principle of Chriftianity,*

Christianity, and that without the couragious asserting thereof, the whole Christian Priest-hood, and the Divine Authority of it, must be called in question, — and encourage every bold Intruder to usurp the Sacred Ministry, in opposition to that Commission, which hath been constantly handed down from Christ and his Apostles to this very day. In the same Place you say you hope, that *none vested with this Divine Authority will fight against it,* &c. which if any Clergy-man should do, in the manner as you there mention, I could not but suspect, that he was one of those who took Gifts and Presents of the *Dissenters,* to let the Names of their Children, who had no other but *Schismatical Lay-Baptisms,* be Registred among the True Baptisms of the Church. This unwarrantable Practise, which you have observed, to be " *scandalously practised in some Places,* I can confirm to be true ; For I knew some Ministers of this City, (now dead) who were guilty of this practise, and are gone to God to give an account of it ; and I my self, soon after I was presented to the Vicarige of *Allhallows Barkin,* had several, and some very great Offers, from *Dissenters,* to enter their Childrens Names, as Baptiz'd, in the Parish Church Register ; and a Parochial Priest of a great City in

b   this

this Kingdom, who gave me a Viſit about a Year ſince, did aſſure me, that all the Miniſters of that Place, himſelf only ex-cepted, were guilty of this execrable pra-ctice; execrable I call it, becauſe it is a double falſification of our *Parochial Dip-tychs*, as they are Regiſters and Records both of Church and State, and I think both Deprivation, and the Pillory to be juſt Puniſhments for that Miniſter, who dares do ſo great and miſchievous a wickedneſs, or ſuffer it to be done.

I ſay, I ſhould be tempted to ſuſpect any Clergy-man, that ſhould write in the manner you mention, againſt you, to be one of that corrupt ſort, or at leaſt of ano-ther, who to court the Favour and Ap-plauſe of the *Diſſenters*, either never Preach in defence of the Church againſt *them*, or if they do, they do it no other-wiſe than barely to ſhew, that the Church of *England* is a *ſafe Communion*, and that thoſe, who through miſtake ſeparated from it, would be in *no danger of Damnation* if they returned to it. But to ſhew that ſeparation from it is 𝕾𝖈𝖍𝖎𝖘𝖒, and by con-ſequence a *damning Sin*, and that the Se-paratiſts of all ſorts from it, are, without the extraordinary mercy of God, in great *and apparent danger of Damnation*, theſe
Gentle-

men love not to touch upon that Point,
nor rife to that Heighth, which long before the Revolution occafioned the diftinction between *High* and *Low* Church men
and the former to be called by ill, or ignorant Men, *High-Flyers, Tantivies,* and
other fuch opprobrious Names. It was,
I fuppofe, a Reflection upon thefe Men,
and the Indignation he had againft their
double practifes, which provoked a Divine
not very many Years fince, to utter a Sarcafm
upon them from the Pulpit, in Words to
this Purpofe, *That fome* (at the time he
fpoke it) *were become Fathers of the Church,
who never were her true Sons.*

Sir, I wifh all Clergy-men, who are concerned in either of thefe Remarks, would
ferioufly confider your pious and feafon-
able Addrefs to us in the conclufion of your
Appendix. We are all concerned, (as you
befeech and conjure us to do,) *to confider
our High and Holy Calling to the Priefthood,* and *to vindicate our unalienable
Rights to adminifter the Holy Sacraments,
and to let the People underftand, that the
Miniftration of them is effential to our
Office, and our Office effential to the Miniftration of them, and that our long and
general filence in not afferting, and defending this great Truth, hath,* as you

obferve,

óbserve, *been the occasion of much ignorance among the People, of the nature of Schism, and the direful consequences of it,* which some of our Order still are, as I am sure some have been, so averse (contrary to their Trust, and the Duty of it) to set before the People. I remember, when some of the *London* Clergy, resolving to do this, as you now beseech us, and for the same Reasons; it was opposed, especially by one of them, for no other reason, but that it would be *censured as Preaching up cur selves*; a Reason, whereof the Weakness and Ill-consequences are shewn by an excellent Person, in the Preface to his *Companion for the Festivals and Fasts of the Church of* England, where, to oblige the Clergy to instruct the People in the great Truth of Sacerdotal Mission, and Authority to administer the Sacraments, He wishes the Catechism of the Church might be continued, in a few Questions and Answers to shew, who only have Power to administer the Holy Sacraments. I need not name this worthy Gentleman, whom God raised up out of the *People* before you, to defend the Rights and Authority of the *Priesthood*, and who thinks it no more diminution, or dishonour to him, to be thought one of *the People* with respect to the *Church*, than one of them with respect to the *State*.

In

In your *Appendix* to your Book, I think you have solidly and satisfactorily answer'd all the Objections that have been made against the useful Subject of it, since the First Edition, taking in your Second Thoughts, and the explanation of your Design, and meaning, in some Passages of it to prevent Offence. This, Sir, is an argument of your great Humility, as well as of your Zeal and Prudence; and your humble and truly Christian Temper and Declaration in *p.* 146, encourage me to make a few Remarks upon your *Appendix*, of which you have the liberty to judge as you please. **P.** 149, you have well observed, *that our Church hath provided no Office of Confirmation* for those, who receive Baptism from *Lay-Baptizers*. And indeed it would have been strange, that she, which allows of no Baptism but by a **Lawful Minister*, should have provided such an Office to confirm, or ratifie the Baptism of those, who truly speaking, were *Sprinkled*, or *Washed*, but not *Baptized*. But I think, you might with reason enough have farther observed, that she hath provided an Office for their true and lawful Baptism. I mean, *Sir*, 𝕿𝖍𝖊 𝕸𝖎𝖓𝖎𝖘𝖙𝖗𝖆𝖙𝖎𝖔𝖓 𝖔𝖋 𝕭𝖆𝖕𝖙𝖎𝖘𝖒 𝖙𝖔 𝖘𝖚𝖈𝖍 𝖆𝖘 𝖆𝖗𝖊 𝖔𝖋 𝖗𝖎𝖕𝖊𝖗 𝖞𝖊𝖆𝖗𝖘 This

---

* *Rubricks in the Ministration of Private Baptism.*

new

new Office was made prefently after *the Restauration*, and is part of the *Liturgy*, that now is confirmed by Act of Parliament. And I do not think it was intended *only* for *Heathens*, *Jews*, and *Mahometans*, who should be converted to Christianity, or for such converted Hereticks among us as reject Baptifm, but also for those who had been *Invalidly Baptiz'd*, of which there were great Numbers at the time of the Reftauration, and now alas! are many more. I fubmit this Obfervation to your Thoughts, and the confideration of all, who fhall read it; and if my Opinion as to this Office is wrong, I hope my Errour is pardonable, becaufe it is not hurtful to the Church, nor cafts the leaft difhonour upon her Learned and Pious Bifhops, and Priefts, her Reprefentatives, who made that Office, which before was wanting. What you there fay of the Paffage in the preceeding Page, concerning *the Validity of Lay Baptifm, viz.* ' that the ' Learned Author never defign'd, that any ' thing in his excellent Book fhould favour ' *Lay Baptifm* in oppofition to the Sacerdo- ' tal power is evidently true, becaufe it is plain from his Words, he means *Lay-Bap-tifm Adminiftred* by *Lay-Men*, fo and fo applied, to dying Perfons, by the Authority

ſity and Allowance of the Church, as in the 38th Canon of the Council of *Eliberis* which you cite *p.* 12. of your *Preliminary Diſcourſe.* And it is very praiſe-woithyinyou that uponSecondThoughts, youcorrectyour ſelf in your Premonition, where you tell us, " *You do not preſume to determine, whether the* " *Church which hath power from Chriſt to* " *give a Man a ſtanding Commiſſion to be a* " *Prieſt, cannot in Caſes of extream neceſſity* " *give him a Commiſſion* pro **hac vice**, (or *pro* " *hic & nunc) to do a* Sacerdotal Act. This Commiſſion of that Council, proceeded, * from an Antient, but a Pious, and inno-cent erroneous opinion, (as I think I may call it) that *Baptiſm was* **abſolutely** *neceſ-ſary to Salvation,* as the communicating of Infants proceeded from another the like-er-roneous belief of the *abſolute* neceſſity of re-ceiving the Holy Euchariſt in order to Sal-vation. This Errour of the abſolute neceſſity of Baptiſm, deſcended in the † Latin Church to after Ages, and acquired ſuch firmneſs of belief by conſtant practiſe, that it re-

---

* Tertull. *de Baptiſmo* Cap xvii. and Voſſium *de Bap-tiſmo Diſput.* xi. v. vi. vii.

† According to the Canon Law . *In neceſſitate quili-bet poſt baptizare, dum modo intendit facere quod Eccle-ſia intendit*

maıned

mained * some time uncorrected by our
Church after the Reformation, but afterwards the Title of the Office for *Private
Baptism* was alter'd thus, 'Of them that are
" to be Baptized in time of necessity by the
" Minister of the Parish, *or any lawful Mi-*
" nister that can be procured; and the Rubrick was accordingly alter'd in this manner," Let the lawful Minister, *and them that
" be present, call upon God for his Grace, and
" say the Lord's Prayer if the time will suffer,
" and then the Child being named by some one
" that is present,* the said lawful Minister
" shall dip it in Water, or pour Water upon
" it, saying these Words, I baptize thee, &c.*
to this change of the Title and Rubrick
of them that are to be Baptized in Private,
(in K. *Edward*'s Book) exactly agrees the
Rubrick of our present Liturgy, cited before in the Margin.

Sir, from these Observations I think I

---

* *As appears from this Rubrick of the Office for them
that be Baptized in Private Houses in time of necessity, in
the Book of Common-Prayer, set forth Anno 2, and 3.
of Edward the Sixth, 1549. The Words of that Rubrick
are these,* First, let them that be present call upon God
" for his Grace, and say the Lord's Prayer, if the time
" will suffer, & then one of them shall name the Child,
' and dip him in the Water, or pour Water upon him,
" saying, I Baptize thee in the Name, &c. vide *Vossium de
Baptismo* X. § x.

may

may conclude, *First*, that the *absolute indispensable* necessity of Baptism is not the Doctrine of the Church of *England. Secondly*, that she approves of no Baptism, or thinks no Baptism duly and validly Administred, but what is Ministred by duly Authorized & lawful Ministers, and consequently that she rejects all *Lay-Baptism. Thirdly*, That she cannot count those duly authorized and lawful Ministers, who take upon them the Ministry within the pale of her Jurisdiction, in contempt of, and opposition to her Episcopat and Episcopal Mission, or Power of Ordination ; and by consequence, that she must look upon Baptism Administred by such Ministers, as Null and Void, from the Beginning. From these Conclusions, and the Consequences issuing from them, I have further reason to think, that the Office of *The Ministration of Baptism to such as are of Riper Years*, was intended for Persons *invalidly Baptized by such unlawful Ministers* among us, as were never duly Authorized, as well as for converted *Heathens, Jews, Mahometans*, and such modern *Manichæans*, and *Seleucians* amongst us, as held it unlawful to Baptize with the Baptism of the Church.

And as you have justly observed, that the learned Author of the passage you cite in *p.* 148. could not design, that any
thing

thing he said in it should favour *Lay-Baptism*: So I dare say for him, that upon Second Thoughts, he will not affirm that it is in the power of the Church to confirm *Ludicrous* Histrionical or other *Mimical Baptisms*, or that any Church or Bishop did ever confirm any of them by Chrism and Imposition of Hands. The Opinion of *Ludicrous Baptism* not to be reiterated, was occasioned by a fabulous Story of *Athanasius*, who, when a little Boy, with others, playing at *Ministers*, as our Children call it, by the Water-side, *Athanasius* acted the *Bishop*, other Boys *Priests* and *Deacons*, and in their Play Baptized several Children, who represented *Catechumens* and *Competents* in form. *Alexander*, Bishop of *Alexandria*, happening to see this, as the Story is told, sent for the Boys, and understanding from their own Relation, that their Ludicrous Baptism was performed by them according to the Rites and Orders of the Church, was of opinion with other Bishops present with him, that the Children so Christned, were not to be Re-baptized, whereupon he confirmed them with Chrism, and Imposition of Hands.

This

This * *Hear-say* Story is told by *Sozomen* from *Ruffinus*, and from him again at large by *Petrus Damianus*, in his Book entituled *Gratissimus*, and mentioned before him by *Watafridus Strabo*, in his Book *de Divinis Officiis*, and reckoned by *Antonius Muretus* in the 9th Chap, of his 13th Book of *various Lections*, among the presages of things that have happened, as Boys have acted them in Play. *Lastly*, such reception this Story of *Athanasius* hath had in the World, that it is cited as true by Dr *George Abbot*, in the Lecture which he read in the Divinity-School at *Oxford*, *de Circumcisione & Baptismo*, 1597, which Lecture he made, to excuse the First Practice of our Church after the Reformation, which he saith *Facilitate larga* with *great Latitude* or *Indulgence* for some time tolerated the Baptism of Lay men and Women in absolute necessity, for the ignorance of the People and hardness of their Hearts. This Story favoured the loose Doctrine of St. *Augustin*, as to the Ministration of Baptism, and therefore we need not wonder that † He spoke

---

' Πεςοῦ ἶτω γνοιάνω τάδε ΦΑΣΙΝ ἐπ ἀυτῶ σὐμ ωβηείναι. Sczа я Ͼ mitt Lib 2 Ch. 17

† D *Laptismo* contra *Donatstas* Lib 7 Versus finem Libri in Tom. 7.

fo

fo favourably of *Ludicrous*, and *Jocular*, as well as *Mimical* and *Hiſtrionical* Baptiſms. But as current as by misfortune this Story hath been, and as many as it hath led into Errour, it is now exploded for very good Reaſons by Learned Men, as by Dr. *Cave* in his *Hiſtoria Literaria*, by *du Pin* in his Notes on *Athanaſe* in his *Nouvelle Bibliotheque*, and by the Learned *Benedictins* in his Life, *p.* 11. Printed before his Works, whither I refer you.

As for *Hiſtrionical Baptiſm* by *Heathens*, that alſo is urged by the Patrons of *Lay-Baptiſm* in favour of their opinion. †Of this they cite this Story out of the *Cronicon Alexandrinum*; that in mockery of the Chriſtians, the Heathen-Players Baptized one of their Companions in warm Water, upon the Stage, and then put upon him a White Garment, upon which he immediately cryed out that he was made a Chriſtian, and would dye as ſuch. The Spectators hearing him declare this, flew upon the Stage, and taking him from thence ſtoned him to death. † *Ado Viennenſis* tells another Story in his Martyrology of *Auguſt.* 25. of St. *Geneſius,* who being Baptized by

† Voſſius de Baptiſmo di *p.* 11. § 29.
† Ibid. cap. 1. § 13

Heathens

Heathens to ridicule Chriftian Baptifm, alfo became a Chriftian : But then fuppofing the truth of thefe Stories, they are as *perfectly miraculous,* as the converfion of fome Pagan Executioners of Martyrs, who declared themfelves Chriftians at the place of Execution, and there fuffered death with them, and were *Baptized in their own Blood.* And therefore, the *miraculous* manifeftation of God's Grace at Hiftrionical Baptifms to teftifie the truth of the Chriftian Religion, and confound its Adverfaries, are no argument for Lay-men to take upon them to Adminifter Baptifm upon any pretence whatfoever. Nay, Sir, fuch an unwarrantable Latitude hath the Church of *Rome* given to the Admiftration of Baptifm, † that fome of her *Popes,* have allowed the Baptifm of *Jews,* and Heathens, and * the Pope in the Council of *Florence* doth exprefly decree, that in *cafe of neceffity* not only a faithful Chriftian *Lay-man,* or *Woman,* but an *Heretick* or *Pagan* may Validly Baptize.

---

† Ibid *Difp* 11. 18
* In decreto Eugenii Papæ ad Armenos: *Minifter hujus Sacramenti eft facerdos, cui ex officio competit Baptizare In Caufa autem neceffitatis, non folum facerdos, vel Diaconus, fed etiam Laicus, vel Mulier, imo etiam Paganus, & Hæreticus Baptizare poteft, &c.*

A 5

As to the cafe of neceffity, fo called, it is, as I have already obferved, founded in the ⸱miftaken opinion of the abfolute neceffity of Baptifm to Salvation. Which Opinion is of Two Sorts, one more antient, grounded on the literal ftrictnefs of the Precept, or inftitution of Baptifm, which was the Errour of *Tertullian*, who therefore in cafe of neceffity, allowed Lay men, but not Women, to Baptize. The other is more modern, as having its rife from the *Pelagian* Controverfy, and that was the indifpenfable neceffity of Baptifm to wafh away Original Sin. This ftrictnefs of opinion, as to the indifpenfable neceffity of this Sacrament, to wafh off the guilt of Original Sin, made St. *Auguftin*, that *durus Pater Infantium*, fo very loofe, as to the Minifter of it in cafe of neceffity. And therefore upon the Queftion, *whether one, who was not a Chriftian, could give Baptifm,* * He delivered his Opinion uncertainly, faying *he would not determine it, becaufe it had not been determined in any Council.* And fo from this Errour of the *abfolute* neceffity of Baptifm to Salvation, the Church of *Rome* came by degrees, to allow the Miniftration of Baptifm by any

---

* *Contra Epift. parmen* Lib. 2. Cap. 13.

Hand,

Hand, when a lawful Minifter could not be had, rather than let a Child perifh, which without it they formerly thought muft be damned, and ftill think cannot be faved, as fuffering *panam aamni,* tho' not *panam fenfus, i. e.* the Lofs of Heaven, tho' not the *Flames* of Hell. * Hence they came *to place all the virtue, and efficacy of Baptifm in the invocation of the Holy Trinity, as in the principal caufe,* not making any difference in the Minifterial, or Inftrumental caufe, in cafe of neceffity. But, Sir, you have fhew'd with great force and clear evidence, that the *Lawful Minifter* is as *effential* to Baptifm, as the Matter, and Form, and cannot be difpenfed with by Men, who are tyed to it by the Divine Inftitution. But though God tyes us, yet he himfelf is not tyed to his own Inftitutions; and therfore the erroneous opinion of the abfolute neceffity of Baptifm by any Minifter, either upon the account of the letter of the Inftitution, or of Original Sin, hath been long rejected by Learned Men, for great, and I think, unanfwer- Reafons, as you may fee in Archbifhop *Bramhalls* Letter to Sir *Henry de Vic,* at

---

* *Decretum Eugenii P. ad Armenos in Conc Florent. Conc. Labb & Coffn. Tom 13. p 535*

the

the 979. p. of his Works, and in the 7 Disp. of *Vossius's* Book *de Baptismo.*

I am extreamly pleased with the modest Reflection you make in your Premonition upon what you had said *p.* 135 of your Book to prove *the Validity of Holy Orders conferred on Unbaptized Persons.* For whereas you distinguish Qualifications for the Ministry, into *Personal* and *Authoritative,* give me leave to tell you, that I think all Qualifications for it are *Personal,* and that of *Personal Qualifications,* the want of *some only* make a Man unworthy of the Ministry, but not uncapable of it ; but the want of others make him utterly uncapable of it, or of being Seperated or Ordained to it. The *Personal* Qualifications of the First sort may be called *Moral,* as Purity, Humility, Sobriety, and all other Vertues and Graces that are comprehended in Holiness of Life, the want of which make a Man unworthy, as of Holy Orders after Baptism, so of Baptism it self, but yet do not Null or make Void either of them, when the Person is Baptized or Ordained. The Second sort of Qualifications are either *Natural, Acquired,* or *Legal,* which last may be also call'd *Political,* as relating to the Fundamental or Positive Laws of the Church. among *acquired* Qualifications

cations we may safely reckon *Reading*, the want of which utterly disables a Man from performing Priestly Offices, and by consequence, makes his Orders Void. Then as for *Natural* Qualifications, they belong either to the *Body* or the *Mind*; to the Body, as speaking, seeing, hearing, the want of which (without any * Canons or Positive Laws of the Church) in my judgment, utterly unqualifies a Man for the Priesthood; and therefore Holy Orders conferred on a Deaf, and Dumb, or Incurable Blind Man, must, in my opinion be Null and Void, because they render him uncapable of performing Ministerial Offices. The like I may say of a Man who wants both his Hands, who though never so worthy upon the score of *Moral Qualifications*, yet, by reason of that natural incapacity, cannot effectually be made a Priest. Qualifications which belong to the *Mind* are Understanding and Memory, the want of which in *Idiots*, *Lunaticks*, and *Maniacs* makes them so utterly uncapable of receiving Holy Orders, that upon supposition, any such were Ordained to the Priesthood, his Orders would be Null and Void. Thus much, Sir, with submission to the

* *Can. Apost.* 69.

c   Learned,

Learned, I have said of Personal Qualifications for the Priesthood, that are Moral,
or Natural. The *Legal* likewise are of
Two Sorts, *First,* such as are *fundamental* to the Christian Society, or Constitution of the Church; or *Secondly,* such as
are super-induced by the *Positive Laws* of
the Church. Of the First sort, in my
Opinion, *Baptism* certainly is, the want
of which therefore I think, must utterly
render a Man uncapable of being a *Christian Priest,* because it makes him utterly
uncapable of *being a Christian,* or of receiving the Holy Eucharist, which to an
Un-baptized Person is θυσία ἄθυτος a Sacrifice
of no more effect than if he had not come
to it; and how then can a Man be made
capable to Administer that Holy Sacrament
to others who hath no right to receive it,
or make others Members of the Church,
of which he is not a Member himself? As
to the latter sort of Legal Qualifications,
the want of which do make a Man uncapable of Holy Orders, and his Orders
Null after he is Ordained, by the Canons
of the Church; I have no occasion to
discourse, and therefore in answer to the
Objection made against you, give me leave
to observe, that I presume it relates to this
case, which is supposed, but never proved
to

to have happened, *viz.* that when a Person *bona fide*, believing himself to have had Valid Priestly Baptism, but indeed had not, yet happens to be Ordained *Bona Fide*, by the Bishop, his Orders notwithstanding are Null and Void. This, I presume, must be the case in which the Objection is put, and not where the Person Ordaining, and the Person Ordained, both *know* that the latter never received any other than *Lay-Baptism*, by one presuming to Baptize in opposition to the Church. these Two Cases are so vastly different, that I believe as to the latter, all *Divines* truly Learned in their profession will make no difficulty to determine, that Orders so conferred are Null and Void. But as to the former case, upon which I take it for granted the Objection proceeds, we must have recourse to *Equity*, which, in such Cases of perfect invincible ignorance, takes place in Ecclesiastical as well as Civil Cases, in Divine as well as Humane Laws. Therefore, Sir, I make no scruple to tell you, that a Priest in this case now before us, is in the Eyes of God a Valid Priest, and that all his Priestly Administrations, are by his allowance also Valid and Effectual, and as acceptable as those of other Priests to him, who can make allowances

C 2   where

where Men cannot, and ratifie what Men, if it came to their knowledge, could not ratifie, but muſt pronounce Null. You know the Prieſthood was hereditary among the *Jews*, and it is not unreaſonable to ſuppoſe, that one Prieſt or other in ſuch a long tract of time might, without any ſuſpicion, have an adulterous Son; upon which ſuppoſition, I believe you will not doubt, that when he was at Age to Adminiſter, God would reckon him among the Prieſts, and accept of all his Adminiſtrations at the Altar; or if ſuch an one happened to be High Prieſt, even in the very *Holy of Holies*, though if his incapacity had been known, he muſt have been depoſed from the Prieſthood.

Sir, in this way of ſtating the Caſe, I am far from encouraging any Perſon ſo Baptized, to take upon him the Prieſthood. For if ſuch an one, knowing himſelf to have no other Baptiſm, offers himſelf to take Holy Orders, I think he commits, a *P*iacular Sin as great as that of *Corah*; nay, if ſuch a one but ſuſpecting himſelf to have no other Baptiſm, takes Holy Orders, I think he commits a Sin of Preſumption, and is obliged to a ſtrict enquiry, whether or no he was ſo Baptized; and if he finds he was, he is bound, as he expects Forgiveneſs

givenefs of God, to cancel his Orders, and abdicate himfelf from the Priefthood. But to prevent either of thefe fuppofeable Cafes, you, like a good Chriftian, have p. 140. inculcated to the Governours of the Church, *how much it is for her fecurity, and ought to be their care, to require of all Candidates of the Miniftry, Certificates of their Baptifm, as well as of their good Converfation*; after which I beg leave to fay, according to my diftinction of Perfonal Qualifications for the Priefthood, that the want of the former makes a Man uncapable to receive Holy Orders, but the want of the latter only makes him unworthy to receive them.

P. 28. You prudently and modeftly decline the great difpute, which exercifed the Church of Old, about the manner of admitting Perfons Baptized in *Herefy* and *Schifm.* You know there was the like difpute among the Apoftles about Circumcifion, and the obfervation of the Mofaick Law, but as St. * *Auguftin* obferves, without any breach of Charity. And as it pleafes God to let the Governours of his Church be fometimes exercifed with great difficulties, fo were they in fome of the Golden

* *Contra Crefconum.* Lib. 2.

c 3

Ages

Ages of it exercifed with this Queftion; but as the fame Father ⁓ obfei ves, *falva unitate,* without dividing the Unity of the Churches. To prove this, he cites the Words of St. *Cyprian* which he fpoke at the opening of the Council of *Carthege,* in which he was at the Head of the moft rigid Side ; to fhew his Moderation in this difpute, of which you may fee a fhort, but clear account, in the Learned Note upon *Meam Sententiam* in 243. *p.* of *Cyprian*'s Works, Printed at *Oxford*, 1382. The Words are thefe, *Supereft, ut de hac ipfa re finguli, quid fentiamus, proferamus, neminem Judicantes, aut a jure Communionis aliquem, fi diverfum fenferit, amoventes.* So in his Epiftle to *Jubaianus,* though he ftrenuoufly and warmly defends his Opinion, yet he concludes with great modefty, and meeknefs, *hæc tibi breviter pro nofta mediocritate refcripfimus, Frater chariffime, neminem præfcribentes, aut prejudicantes, quo minus unusquifque Epifcoporum, quod putat faciat, habeas arbitrii fui liberam poteftatem. Nos quantum in nobis eft*

⁓ Ibid *Neque enim part. momenti, quod inter Epifcopos Avrei ioiis Ætatis quam effe me putat Pars Donati, ifta quæftio fluduavit, & varias habuet inter fe Collega---- falva Divina Sciten ia.*

propter

propter *Hæreticos cum Collegis & Co-Episcopis nostris non contendimus, cum quibus Divinam Concordiam, et dominicam pacem tenemus, maxime cum & Apostolus dicat, si quis autem putaverit contentiosus esse, nos talem consuetudinem non habemus, neque Ecclesiæ Dei.* These Passages plainly shew, that the Peace and Unity of the Church was not to suffer in this contention, but that the Bishops and Churches of both Sides were * to be left to their own Customs, and the Practice of their Fathers, as St. *Basil* speaks in his First Canonical Letter to *Amphilochius*, Bishop of *Iconium*, about the Baptism of the *Novatians*. Indeed, there was no reason why the Bishops should divide Communion, and break the Unity of the Episcopal College in this Controversy; because, *First*, both Parties agreed in their Sentiments, of the direful sacrilegious, and damnable Nature of *Heresy* and Schism, and particularly of the Schism made by the *Novatians*, and *Donatists*. *Secondly*, they both run back, and unravelled the Successions of their *Antibishops* to Interruptions, *optatus Milev.* in the one, as well as *Cyprian* in the other

---

* ὅτι δεῖ τῷ ἔθει τῶν καθ ἑκάςην Χῶραν ἕπεσθαι.
⸸ Lib. 2 P 36, 37.

C 4   Schism

Schism. *Thirdly*, both compared them to *Corah*, *Dathan*, and *Abiram*, and likewise to Adulterers, and looked upon their Ordainers as Traditors. And *lastly*, both asserted, that in those Schisms none could be saved in the ordinary way, without returning to the Church. But then, though they agreed in the charge of Schism, they differed as to the manner of reconciling *Schismaticks* ; one side being for Baptizing those again who were Baptized in Schism, because they thought their Baptism to be * *Null*, *Extraneous*, and *Profane*, and that Schismatical Churches were † only like Churches, but were not real Churches, and by consequence, that their Bishops, and Priests, could not Validly Baptize, or do any other Priestly Act. Therefore they had one way of reconciling Penitents, who had been Baptized in the Church, when they returned to it from the Schism, and another of re-

---

* Cypr *Epist.* 71, 72, 73 *Edit* Oxon.

† Cyprianus Jubaiano *Quando ad nos non omnino ut licet, quid Hostes Ecclesiæ faciunt, dummodo teneamus ipsi potestatis nostra honorem, & rationis, ac veritatis firmamentum. Nam Novatianus suarum more, quæ cum Honore non sint, Homines tamen mutantur, sicut Ecclesiæ Catholicæ autoritatem sibi, & Honorem vindicare, quando ipse ab Ecclesia venit imo adhuc insuper contra Ecclesiam Rebellis & Hostis existunt.*

conciling

conciling those who had been Baptized in the Schism, when they came over to the Church. The former they only looked upon as * *Stray-Sheep*, and as such re-admitted them into the Fold barely by imposition of Hands. But they looked upon the latter as *Non Oves*, who did not belong to the Fold, and were not Sheep at all, and therefore determined that they ought to be Baptized in the Holy Catholick Church, that they might become Sheep of her Fold.

The other side on the contrary, though they looked upon those Schismatical Churches not to belong to the *Holy Catholick Church*, but to be extraneous to it, and alienated from it, yet they looked upon them as Parts, though as factious, sacrilegious Parts of the Universal Church, which were guilty of the highest breach of

* *Quod nos quoque Domino offerimus, ut quos constat hic Baptizatos esse, & a nobis ad Hæreticos transisse, si possint uno peccato suo cognito, & crimine ducto, ad veritatem & Matricem venire, latius in Pænitentiam Manum imponere, ut quia ovisfuerat sanc Ovem ac alienatam & erraturam in Ovile suum Pastor recipiat, si autem quis ab Hæreticis venit, Baptizatus in Ecclesia prius non fuit sed alienus in totum, & profanus venit, Latizandus est, ut Ovis fiat, quia unica est aqua in Ecclesia sancta, quæ Oves facit.* Cyprian, Epist. ad Quintum.

Charity,

Charity, and compared them to the * Veffels of difhonour in the Houfe of God.
I fay, they looked upon them as Parts of
the Univerfal Church, in the moft extended fenfe of the Word as it comprehends
Good, and Bad, Sound and Corrupt, Orthodox, and Hæretical, Pure, and Adulterous Churches, Churches under, and
Churches free from the charge of Schifm,
and as Members of the Univerfal Church
in the largeft fenfe they alfo looked upon
them as *real* Churches, and the Miniftrations of their Bifhops, and Priefts, and
the Sacraments they Adminiftred, as *good
in themfelves*, though *unprofitable*, becaufe,
both Givers, and Receivers, wanted Charity, as being divided from the Unity of
the Church. This St. *Auguft.* inculcates
again and again of † Schifmatical Baptifm,

---

* Auguft. *Donatiftis Epift.* 166. *Perne eos non vult
Deus in facrilega difcordia alienatos a Matre veftra Catho-
lica,* Contra Donatift. L·b. 1. *Qui feparationis aperto Sacrilegio manifefti funt ; Eos iterum a* Sacrilegio Schifmatis
revocat.

† *Auguft.* in Evang. Johan. *Tract* 6. *Et poteft fieri, ut
aliquis habeat Baptifmum præter columbam . ut profit ei Bap-
tifmus, præter columbam non poteft —— docet nos colum-
ba, refpondet enim de capite Domini, dicens, Baptifmum habes, charitatem autem, qua Ego Gemo non habes Quid eft
hoc, nequit, Baptifmum habeo, charitatem non habeo. Sacra-
mentum habeo, Charitatem non. Noli clamare, oftende mihi
quomodo habeat charitatem, qui dividit unitatem. ego, in-*

where

where he defends the *Validity of it in it
self.* And as Martyrdom out of the Unity is unprofitable to Salvation, so he saith,
Baptism is. The Fathers of the *Latin*
Church, particularly the *Africans*, in St.
Augustin's time looked upon *Schism*, and
the utter violation of Charity in it, as

---

quit, *habeo Baptismum : habes, sed* sine charitate nihil tibi
prodest. *Baptismi quippe aliquid est, & magnum aliquid
est propter illum, dequo dictum est, hic est qui Baptizat, sed
ne putaras illud quod magnum est tibi* aliquid prodesse posse
si non fueris in Unitate. —— *Si Baptismum habes esto in Co-
lumba, ne non tibi prosit, quod habes, veni ergo ad columbam dicimus, non ut incipias habere, quod non habebas, sed
ut prodesse tibi incipiat, quod hales.* Foris *enim habebas
Baptismum ad perniciem;* intus *si habueris,* incipit prodesse
ad salutem. Contra Epist. parmeniani. Lib. 2. *aliud
est prorsus non habere, aliud perniciose habere, aliud salubriter habere, quicquid non habetur dandum est, cum opus
est dari, quod vero perniciose habetur per correctionem de-
pulsa pernicie agendum est, ut* salubriter habeatur Contra
Crescon. Gramm. Lib 2. *Ita vobis & nos dicimus, quem
Baptismum vos ignorantes observatis, ejus potestatem vobis
nos annunciamus, non ut cum ad nos veneritis alterum acci-
piatis, sed ut eum, qui jam apud vos erat,* utiliter accipi-
atis. Contra Donatistos, Lib. 1. *Non eis itaque dicimus, nolite dare, sed* nolite in Schismate dare. *Nec eis
quos videntur baptizaturi, dicimus, nolite accipeti, sed nolite in Schismate accipere.* —— *Si postea venire ad
Catholicam cogitat, quia certus est ibi prodesse Sacramen-
tum, quod alibi accipi quidem potest,* prodesse autem non
potest. —— *In Ecclesia Baptismum* recte accipi, — *Non
autem illic (apud Donatistos)* recte accipi. Augustin de
Bapt. contra Donatistos, Lib. 4. *Ecclesia paradiso compa-
rata indicat nobis, posse quidem ejus Baptismum Homines
etiam foris accipere, sed salutem beatitudinis extra eam ne-*

an impedient Cause, which hinder'd the descent, and the reception of the Holy Spirit upon the Baptized in Schism, and their receiving the *Grace of the Sacrament*, which only could make the Sacrament effectual to Salvation; and upon the whole, Sir, I cannot but observe, that the difference between the *Nullity* & *Inutility* of Schismatical Baptism is not very great, if it be considered, that those Words are so nearly allyed to one another, that in the *Civil Law*, the Latter is often used to signifie the Former, so *inutilis Stipulatio* signifies a void Bargain, and *inutiliter testari* to make a *Will* that is Void, or *no Will* And so the *Inanis* of St. *Cyprian*, and *Inutilis* of St. *Augustin*, let them differ as they will, are both so terrible, that either of them methinks should fright *Schismaticks* from the sad State they are in, to

---

minem vel percipere, vel tenere. ——— *Eos (Hæreticos) doceamus, quod ex unitate habent, non valere ad salutem, nisi ad eandem venerint unitatem.* ——— *Salus (inquit) extra Ecclesiam non est, quis negat?* Et ideo quæcunque ipsius Ecclesiæ habentur extra Ecclesiam non valent ad salutem, sed aliud est non habere, aliud non utiliter habere. De Unit. Ecclef. *Sacramenta eadem funt, sed* non profunt, *qui cum illis recta sint, ipsi perversi sunt.* ——— *Accipiat vinculum pacis, quod non habebat, sine quo illi prodesse non poterit Baptisma quos habebat.* ——— *Baptismus autem in eo, qui justitiam non habet, esse potest, sed* non potest prodesse.

betake

betake themſelves to the Ark and Sanctuary of the Church, and be reconciled to her,
either by reiterated Baptiſm, as St. *Cyprian*
ſaith many Thouſands were in his time, or
only by *Impoſition of Hands*, which afterwards obtained in the *Latin* Church.
Wherefore, Sir, I agree with you, that
the manner of admitting, and reconciling ſuch Penitent Schiſmaticks, as returned from the *Novatians* and *Donatiſts*,
ought not now to be matter of diſpute.
For the converſion of ſuch is the main
Point, and the manner of admitting them
ought to be left to the cuſtom of Churches.

Here I cannot but obſerve to you, with
what † *Lenity and Gentleneſs* the Church
of *Africa* treated the *Donatiſts*. * *She
allowed their Ordinations as well as Baptiſms*,
and in a Dioceſs where there was a Church-
Biſhop, and a Donatiſt Biſhop, *She offered
a Partition of ſuch a Dioceſs, in which the
Senior of them ſhould divide, and the Ju-
nior chooſe. * She alſo received the Clergy men among the *Donatiſts* upon their
Converſion, to the ſame honour that
they enjoyed among the *Donatiſts*, * and
alſo admitted thoſe who were Baptized in

---

† African Code *in the Clergy-man's Vade mecum. Part*.
*Can. 66. * Can 69. * Can. 118. † Can. 68. * Can. 47. 57.*
their

their Infancy by the *Donatifts*, not only into the Church but alfo *to the Miniftry of the Altar, when they were converted, and had received Impofition of Hands.* Without Converfion and Admiffion into the Unity, to which the Church Bifhops invited them by thefe Conceffions and Honours, there could be no reunion, or making the Two into one Communion again. But the *Donatift* Bifhops having Numbers, and Strength on their Side refufed, and flighted all the Offers of the Church, and fo added Obftinacy and Contempt to their Sin. * St. *Augaftin* tells us they were fo proud & uncondefcending, that they would not come to any pacifick Conference with them, (*till forc'd by the Emperour*) but prided themfelves in their Schifm. Sir, I have referred you above to the Canons of the *African Code*, as they are abridged in the Second Part of the *Vade Mecum*, becaufe I had a mind to notifie that excellent and ufeful Book to the

---

+ Exhort *ad* Concord Ecclef *Epift* 166. *Nihil in nos aliquando probare potuiftis, refti Epifcopi conventi a nobis, nunquam pacifice cum nobis conferre voluerunt, quafi fugientes cum peccatoribus loqui. Quis ferat iftam fuperbiam, quafi Paulus Apoftolus non contuler t cum peccatoribus, & cum ipfe facrilegis Quid ipfe Dominus non cum Iudæis a quibus crucifixus eft, Sermones de lege habuerit. ——ut intelligatos ipfos idem nobifcum nolle conferre, quia caufam fuam perd. ...*

World,

World, for which the Author deserves great praise and thanks. But Sir, nevertheless I desire you, who understand *Latin*, to read them at large in that Language, in *Justel's Bibliotheca Juris Canonici veteris, Tom* 1. and when you have leasure the Conferences at *Carthage* between the *Catholicks*, and the *Donatists* in *Optatus Milevitanus's* Works, or rather St. *Augustins Breviculum* of them in the 7th Vol. of his Works.

I have observed to you in the beginning of my Letter, that as there never was any Church founded, but *in* and *with* Episcopacy, so no Sect ever assumed the Title of a Church, till they had a pretended rightful Bishop, before the time of the Reformation So *essential* did all Christians (till that time) think Bishops to the Church *as a Society,* according to that of St. *Cyprian* in * his 66. Epist " *Illi sunt Ec-* " *clesia Plebs Sacerdoti adunata, & Pastori* " *suo Grex adhærens. Unde scire debes Epis-* " *copum in Ecclesia esse, & Ecclesiam in Epis-* " *copo, & si qui cum Episcopo non sint, in* " *Ecclesia non esse.* A Church is composed " of the People united to the Bishop, and the

---

* *Edit. Oxon.*

Flock

" *Flock adhering to their Paftour, therefore*
" *you ought to know, that the Bifhop is in the*
" *Church, and the Church in the Bifhop ; fo*
" *that they who are not with the Bifhop are*
" *not in the Church.*

This is exactly according to the Apo-
ftolical Doctrine of St. *Ignatius.* But, Sir,
to fhew you, or rather the Reader, that all
Sects, who defired to be accounted Churches, were headed by Bifhops *as Principles of
Unity,* I need but inftance in the *Montanifts,*
thofe antient *Camifars,* who being condemned by the whole Catholick Church, formed
themfelves into a feperate Church, over
which they pretended to fet *Bifhops* and
Presbyters, whom they chofe out of the *Pro-
phetical Order,* as in the time of the Apoftles,
by the *Immediate Call* of God, I mean by the
exprefs defignation of the *Holy Ghoft,* or
a vifible manifeftation of the Divine Un-
ction refting upon them. They alfo fet
up a Primat in the fame manner over their
New Church, which they declared to be
the moft perfect that ever had been on the
Face of the Earth. This, *Sir,* you may
fee in the Hiftory of *Montanifm, in One of
the Three Difcourfes* newly Publifhed againft
our pretended new Prophets, to which I refer you ; and it is natural to conclude, that
they either had no notion of a Church
without

without *Bishops*, or that they feared to be detected as false Prophets for rejecting the Apostolical Order, and therefore according to the practise of the Catholick Church unto that time, from which they durst not depart, they founded their New Churches *in* and *with* Episcopacy; of all which they looked upon the Church of *Pepuza*, a City of *Phrygia*, to be the Mother, as *Hierusalem* was of the *Catholick Church*.

My next Instance shall be in *Novatian*, the Founder of the *Novatian* Schism, who got himself to be Ordained by Three unworthy Bishops in such an indirect and scandalous manner, as you may read in the 43d Ch of the 6th Book of the Ecclesiastical History of *Eusebius*. According to this received Principle of the necessity of a Bishop to a Church, most of the Troubles in the Ancient Churches were not for *pulling down Bishops*, but about *setting of them up*, that every Party might have a Bishop for a pretended Principle of Unity; and so the *Novatians*, though they were divided from the Church for a long time, yet maintained an Episcopal Succession, that they might in all Places have the Form and Fashion, and Appearance of a Church. Thus the Party of the *Donatists* in *Africa*, so called from *Donatus* a *Casis Nigris*, who began

d

to trouble the Church in the time of *Men*
surius, Primate of *Carthage*, after his Death
set up *Majorinus* against *Cæcilian*, his next
lawful Successor, who had been truly E-
lected and Consecrated into his Place.
They knew the People of that City would
not follow them without a Bishop, and
having by that means formed a mighty
Party there, they were headed by * those
other Bishops who condemned *Cæcilian*
and set up *Majorinus* against him, and
thereby formed the most deplorable Schism
that ever was in any of the Churches of
Old. The People then had no notion of a
Church without a Bishop, (unless in a vacant
Church where the Altar continues) much
less of a Church set up against *Episcopacy.* For
had they thought that a Church could be
without a Bishop, and Episcopal Successors
the Misleaders of them at any time into
Heresy or *Schism*, need not have taken so
much pains, or used so many indirect Arts
to be made Bishops, but have set up *Pres-*
byterian Churches, which was so contrary
to *Catholick* Practise, and the *common*
Principle of Bishops being the Apostles
Successors, and Principle of Unity in the
respective Churches, that they either never thought of doing it, or if they did
they thought they could never do it with

* Henricus vates de Schismate Donatistarum Cap
succe

fuccefs. So in the famous fub divifion from the Church among the *Donatifts,* which feperated from them as they had feperated from the Church, * *Maximianus* a factious Deacon, was fet up by them, againft *Primianus* their Bifhop of *Carthage,* as they at firft fet up *Majorinus* againft *Cæcilian:* which they need not have done, if a Church without a Bifhop would have ferved their turn. This Sect of the *Maximianifts* is mentioned in that memorable Canon of the *African Code,* wherein the Fathers Ordained, that Legates fhould be fent to preach Peace to the *Donatifts,* both Clergy and People, and to fhew them, that they departed from the Church as unjuftly as the *Maximianifts* divided from them, and that they fhould alfo be exhorted to receive Converts from the *Maximianifts,* as the Church did from them, *viz. allowing their Ordination and Baptifm.*

But, Sir, to fhew thofe who know not the Story, how the Principle of Epifcopacy was tranfmitted to latter Ages, and kept its ground to the 15th Century, permit me to relate the Opinion and Proceedings of the *Presbyters* of thofe *Bohemians* and *Moravians,* who in perfecution retiring to a Mountainous Country near *Silefia,* grew

---

* Auguft. *de Geftis cum* Emerifto *Donatift. Epifcop.*

very

very follicitous how the People fhould have
the Miniftry continued unto them after
they were dead. * In this deliberation they
had fome thoughts, which neceffity fugge-
fted to them of ordaining other Presbyters
to fucceed them. But fearing that fuch Ordinations would not be Legitimate nor de-
fenfible, if called in queftion, at length in
the Year 1467. the moft eminent among
them that were difperfed through *Bohemia*
and *Moravia*, met together to the Number
of about 70, who addreffing themfelves to
God with Frayers and Tears, befeeched
him to fhew them if their Purpofe were
agreeable to his holy Will, and if that
were the time for it, and then proceeded in the following manner to know
the Will of God by *Lot*. They chofe
by Suffrages *Nine Men* from among themfelves, whom they thought moft worthy
to be *Bifhops*, and having put into the
Hands of a Child *Twelve* little Papers fold-
ed up, they directed him to diftribute them
among the *Nine* Perfons Nine of the Papers

* Ecclefiæ Sclavonicæ Bohemæ in Gente potiffimum radi-
catæ Hiftoriola. § 59, 60, 61. *fed quaffabat animos me-
tus, an fatis legitima foret Ordinatio, fi Presbyter presby-
terum crearet, non vero Epifcopus? et quomodo talem Ordi-
nationem, fi his moveatur defenfum effent, five apud ali-
fui apud fuos.*

we

were *Blank*, and on the other Three only were written E S T, *it is*, to wit, *the Will of God*, which they had begg'd him to diſcover to them. It might have ſo happened, that every one of the *Nine* Perſons might have got a *Blank Paper*, which would have been a ſign to them of the *Negative Will* of God. But it came to paſs, that the *Three Written Papers* fell into the Hands of Three among them, who were noted for their Piety, Learning, and Prudence.

Theſe * they embraced with joy, as given unto them from Heaven, and then deliberated about their Conſecration. And to that End ſent Three of their Miniſters to a part of the *Waldenſes*, who being baniſhed out of *France*, came to reſide in the Confines of *Auſtria* and *Moravia*. To theſe they related their ſad State, and having asked their Counſel, *Stephanus*, one of their Biſhops, calling to him another Biſhop, and ſome Miniſters, he made known to them the purity of their Doctrine, the grievous Perſecutions they had ſuffered in *France* and *Italy*, and * *the law-*

π *Ibid §. 60.*
* *Cumque dicti* Waldenſes *legitimos ſe habere Epiſcopos legitimamque, & non interruptam ab Apoſtolis uſque ſucceſſionem affirmarent, creavunt tres e noſtrorum Miniſtris Epiſcopos,* &c. *In præfat. Ante Rationem diſciplinæ in Unitate Fratrum Bohemorum.*

ful

ful uninterrupted Succession of their Bishops from the first Plantation of Christianity among them to that time. To them therefore the *Bohemian* Ministers, Elected by Lot, were sent to be Consecrated Bishops, after which they resolved to unite with the *Waldenses,* who were suddenly scattered by a new Persecution, in which, *Stephan.* their Bishop suffered Martyrdom, being inhumanely burnt at *Vienna.* † *Joh. Amos Comenius* was the last Bishop of this *Bohemian* Succession, who lived to see the † utter ruine of the *Bohemian* and *Moravian* Churches, occasioned by their impatience * under the *Cross,* in taking up *Arms* against their Lawful Sovereign, and setting up another against him.

But having mentioned *Colluthus* above, as an Usurper upon the Episcopal Office in presuming to Ordain *Presbyters,* give me leave to tell the Story, because, as Lawyers speak, it is a *Book-case,* which shews the Invalidity of *Presbyterian Ordination.* This *Colluthus,* a Presbyter of *Alexandria,* took

---

† Joh Amos. *Comenei Dedicatorium Alloquium* p 8,9,10.
* *Hoc egerunt ut cas exquisitis e'vexationibus ad impatientiam, & dehinc ad* Arma, *proitarent.*
† *Eo res deducta est, ut intra* Bohemiam, & Moraviam *nullum amplius Evangelicis Templum, nulla Schola, nullum privatum Religionis Exercitium.* &c.

upon

upon him in oppofition to his Bifhop to Ordain certain *Presbyters*, and among the reft one called * *Ifchyras*, who accufed *Macarius*, a Presbyter of *Athanafius*, for breaking the Chalice while he was Adminiftring at the Holy Altar ; and this fcandalous Story was one of thofe which the *Arians* invented, and brought againft *Athanafius*, and were all examined, and found to be Lyes by a great † Council, which met at *Alexandria* in the Year of our Lord, 340. As to this particular Story, the Council upon enquiry declared * *Firft* , that in the Place where the *Holy Cup* was faid to be broken by *Macarius* , there was no Church, *Secondly*, nor Presbyter there to Adminifter, nor *Thirdly*, was the Day in which the Fact was faid, a Day of Communion, nor *Laft* of all was *Ifchyras* a Prieft, * being only Ordained by *Colluthus*, *who dyed a Presbyter, and whofe Impofition of Hands* was of no Authority, or Validity, and that, all who were Ordained by him, were Laymen, and communicated in the Affem-

---

* ποτήριον μυρεκόν
† Athanaf. *Apol.* 2.
† ‘Αλλ’ οτι μηδὲν ἦ ὅλως ἐκεῖ πῶς γάρ ; ὅτω μήτε τόπος κυριακῆς μήτε τις ἐκεῖ Εκκλησίας αλλα μήτε ὁ καιρὸς μυσηρίων ἦν

* Αλλ’ ὅτι ΚΟΛΛΟΤΟΘ)Σ πρεσβυτερος ὢν ἐτελευτήσε, καὶ πάντα Χεὶς αὐτῶ γίνονεν άχυρος, &c.

blies

blies as fuch. To this Teftimony of the
Church, let me add another of a *Spanifh*
Bifhop, who having fore Eyes at an Ordination of Prefbyters only laid his Hands
upon them, fuffering a Prefbyter to read
the Words of Ordination. This coming
to be debated in the * Second Council of
Sevil, was, upon mature deliberation, thus
determined. *Firft*, that the Prefbyter,
had he been alive, fhould have been cen-
fured for his prefumption. And *Secondly*,
that the Prefbyters and Deacons, fo Ordained, fhould be depofed from their Sacred Orders, which they had wrongfully
received. This fhews, that this Council
were of opinion, that *Prefbyters* could have
no *Effential* Part in Ordination, and therefore, that they are liable to cenfure, merely
for reading the Words of Ordination, which
formally conftitute a *Prefbyter*, or *Deacon*,
though with the allowance of his Bifhop,
who is not fuppofed to have power to Authorize him to do that, which he only
hath Authority to do himfelf

Upon what you have Written, P. 57.
about the *Form of Baptifm*, 𝕴𝕟 𝕥𝕙𝕖
𝕹𝕒𝕞𝕖 𝕠𝕗 𝕥𝕙𝕖 𝕱𝕒𝕥𝕙𝕖𝕣, &c. Sir, give me
leave to recommend to your perufal, what
is written by a very Learned Divine, and

* *Concil. Hifp.* 11. *Cap.* 5.

an old Sufferer for the Church of *England*, Mr. *Christopher Elderfield* in his Book of *Regeneration* and *Baptism*, from P. 183. to P. 207.

I cannot but declare my consent to what you have written, P. 133. *viz.* That *supposing it were (as it is not) possible, for the Church to be deprived at once of all her Bishops, it would be our duty, as well as safety, in that Destitution, to Wait and Pray, and hope for a new Revelation of the Will of God, rather than to take upon our selves to make Bishops, for which we ha e no Authority.* And I concur with you also in your Conclusion, P. 134. That *no Doctrine whatsoever, can be proved false,* [*or as I beg leave to add ought to be rejected*]*because Numbers of Men may be involved in the sad Consequences that arise from it.* To which let me also add, more especially, when they are involved in them, contrary to their Knowledge, or by their own wilful Ignorance, or Mistake, or by Worldly Interest, and evil Passions. This, *Sir*, will appear plainly, if we consider the *received Principles* of Christianity, which are either Speculative, or Practical, that is, either Doctrines or Commands. By the *Speculative* Principles, I mean all the received Doctrines of Faith, which we are bound to believe in order to Salvation,

and

and by the *Practical*, thofe, which oblige us to fome Practical Duty, which are again of three Sorts, *Moral, Ritual,* and *Political.* And there are none of thefe Principles, which fome Men among us, in this Age of Deftructive Latitude, will not give up, or ftrive to bend, and relax, for fear, or favour, when great Numbers of Men, efpecially of Men in power, are concerned in the Confequences of them. To inftance in one of the Speculative Principles : You cannot but know, that fome do not like our Preaching up the Doctrine of *Chrift's being God,* or, *God of God,* of the fame *Effence,* or *Subftance* with the Father, and the Belief of it, as neceffary to Salvation, becaufe fo many *Arians,* and *Socinians,* and other unexcufable Unbelievers are involved in the dangerous Confequences of that Doctrine ; and for their fakes, and, it may be, fecretly for their own, they rack their Inventions to find out new, loofe, and Evafive Expofitions of that Fundamental Myftery to Chriftianity, and exprefs them in odd uncertain Terms un known to all *Antiquity,* and as different in Senfe, as in Sound from the Language of the *Catholick Church.* I have faid, *in-excufable* Unbelievers, though thefe Gentlemen of large thoughts, and pretended

large

large Charity would excuſe them, becauſe the Myſtery is incomprehenſible, and
the manner of the thing, as taught by,
the Catholick Church, unconceivable by
Humane Underſtanding : But let me
ſay, no otherwiſe unconceivable by us,
than ſome *Natural Myſteries* are, which
though we cannot conceive, yet we believe.
They will tell us in behalf of theſe Unbelievers, that Mens Minds are as different
as their Faces, that our Brains, and the
Cells in them, are of different make, and
that all Men cannot believe alike. But,
Sir, to ſhew the Vanity of ſuch Apologies,
let us ſuppoſe, that ſome of our Country-
men were Trading among a People very
remote from the Sea, imagine under the
foot of Mount *Caucaſus,* and had told
them, that the Waters of the River,
which run through the Capital City of
England, did twice every day, and ſometimes
oftner, run backwards up the ſame Channel,
down which the Stream had run not long
before, and that the *King* of that People, as
well as the People, wondring at this relati·
on ſhould ſend Letters to the *Queen* to deſire
her Majeſty, that if it was true, ſhe would
be pleaſed to confirm the Truth of it by an
Anſwer with her *Royal Seal,* and that,
after he received her *Majeſty*'s moſt Au-
thentick

thentick Letter, fhould neverthelefs declare he would not believe *the thing*, becaufe he could not conceive the manner of it, nor how it could poffibly be done, and thereupon alfo did brand the Firft Relators of this unconceivable natural Myftery, as *Lyars*, and then banifh them out of his Dominions. Suppofing all this, Sir, do you think it were reafonable, to make an Apology for fuch a Princes obftinate incredulity, who, upon the Authority of fuch Teftimonies, would not believe the thing, becaufe it was not only above his Underftanding, but that of all the Philofophers in his Kingdom. I fay, would it be reafonable, for fuch a Prince, and his Philofophers, to dis-believe, or doubt of that thing after fuch undoubted Humane Authority for the truth of it, or for others to Palliat, or Excufe their obftinate Unbelief, becaufe Men's Minds are not all alike, and their Brains of different make. Sir, I wifh the Gentlemen, for whofe fake I have made this comparifon, would confider it, and no longer, under pretence of *Univerfal Charity*, and the *different Features of Minds*, write in fuch manner of the great Myftery of our Religion, as to confirm our Doubters, or Unbelievers in their Scepticifm, or Unbelief, and thereby give them occafion

fion to reject it as uncertain or falfe, rather than be involv'd in the dreadful confequence of their Unbelief, fhould it be, as it certainly is, a Divine Truth.

Then as to the Practical Principles, which I call Precepts, or *Commands*, they are alfo as neceffary to be *obferved* as the other are to be *believed*; and if I may fo fpeak, are as dear to God as any Article of Faith, and yet there is none of them, which fome Men of *Latitude* among us will not foften, and trim up into another fenfe, to pleafe the Tranfgreffors of them to their Eternal Ruin.

Thus, Sir, that very Sect, which not only neglects, but defpifes the Two Sacraments as Temporary Inftitutions, or Ritual Ordinances, appointed only for the *Infant-State* of the Church, are not only allowed the Title of Chriftians, but reckoned in the ordinary State of Salvation by fome free thinkers in the *Broad Way*, which leadeth to Deftruction. And then, as to the *Political Doctrines*, or Principles, relating to the Government of the Church, though it was the confentient Belief of all Chriftians for Fifteen Hundred Years, that Bifhops were the Succeffors of the Apoftles, & as fuch only have power to Ordain Minifters in the Church, yet have we
Men

Men, and Men of no ordinary Figures in the Church, that not only never Preach this Doctrine themselves, but do not love that others should Preach it, or Instruct the Youth in it, because say they, *it Un-churches the Foreign Churches.* But, Sir, in the Name of God, is it this received Principle of the *Catholick Church*, that Unchurches Foreign Churches, or do they Unchurch themselves in continuing wilful Transgressors of it ? As not to speak more of the *Moral Principles* of Christianity, is it for instance, the Doctrine of Sobriety, or Justice, or Temperance, or Purity, or Humility, that damns so many Millions of Christians, or do they damn themselves by their wilful violation of them ? The Positive Laws of God are all Sacrosanct, *especially those he hath Ordain'd for Government*, and he will in no wise excuse the wilful Neglect, Contempt, or Transgression of them ; but every such Transgression and Disobedience against the Polity of the Christian Theocracy, let the Number of Offenders be never so great shall receive a just Recompence of Reward. And therefore judge, *Sir*, who act most like Primitive Christians, and the faithful Servants of Christ, *those*, who in all Meekness, and Charity, set this received Prin-

ciple

ciple concerning the *Oecumenion Theocracy* of the Myftical *Ifrael,* the Neceffity of Conformity and Obedience, and the Confequences of Difobedience to it before the *other* Churches, or thofe, who footh and flatter them in their Errour, becaufe they are *whole Nations,* though moft of them have abandoned the Divine Order of Bifhops, purely for Human Reafons of State, and particularly becaufe they have alienated the Revenues, by which they were maintained. Yet, *Sir,* the fame Perfons, who had rather this *Principle* were fupprefs'd, than that thofe Nations fhould, as they fpeak, be *Unchurched* by it, would, at leaft many of them, make no difficulties to *Unchurch* leffer Bodies of Chriftians by it, and let the Confequences which arife from it, have their full force upon a few, though the Tranfgreffion *of the Principle,* and the Confequences of the Tranfgreffion equally affect a great, as well as a fmall Number, and condemn whole Nations of Chriftians as much, and as effectually as fingle Men. But thefe Gentlemen fhould confider that they are the Multitudes and great Numbers that will be condemned at the Day of Judgment. Furthermore, *Sir,* You know, what indifpenfable Obligations, lye upon all Chriftians, and Chri

ftian

ſtian Nations, to *profeſs the Faith once de-livered to the Saints, and to contend earneſt-ly for it*, and accordingly how carefully it was guarded, and how zealouſly contend-ed for againſt all Hereticks, who from the Beginning oppoſed it, or any part of it : and therefore, if we muſt believe and contend for *Divine Revelations*, which have always been oppoſed, why ſhould we not as zealouſly obſerve and contend for that *Divine Inſtitution*, which was never oppoſed for 1500 Years, I mean, that Form of Government, which all Chri-ſtianity received and Practiſed for ſo many Ages, as that only Eccleſiaſtical Polity, which was appointed by Chriſt to continue unto the End of the World.

Sir, I have taken occaſion from your Aſſertion to ſay thus much in behalf of *Epiſcopacy*, as a *received Principle of Chri-ſtianity*, and from thence to ſhew, how it concerns all our Divines, eſpecially of the Epiſcopal Order, to ſet the dangerous con-ſequences of rejecting it before the *Foreign Churches*, and thereupon to invite, encou-rage, and exhort, nay to Conjure them in the Name of Chriſt, to join the Apoſtoli-cal Government to the Apoſtolical Faith of the Church, that thereby they may become wholly Pure and Primitive, and

not

not only in part, but in whole, as we are, and all Chriftian Nations ought to be. This furely, would better become the Men of higher Stations and Characters in the Church, than, in finful complaifance to Foreign Churches, to condemn Books of moft excellent inftruction for the younger fort *at School*, becaufe they teach them, that *Bifhops were Succeffors to the Apoftles in the Church, and only have power to ordain, and fend forth Labourers into God's Vineyard.* Thefe Gentlemen furely forget, that as the nature of the Church, as a *Sect*, confifts in Doctrines; So, as fhe is a *Society*, it confifts in that frame of Polity which God hath Ordained for the Government thereof. wherefore, inftead of condemning, they fhould rather recommend all fuch Books, as Inftruct the *Laity*, Young, or Old, in Primitive Chriftianity, and encourage them to read all fuch Tracts, and Difcourfes in their own or any other Tongue, as will give them true Views of the State of the Primitive Church in the Beft and Pureft Ages, and of the Manners of the Primitive Chriftians in them; and were this diligently done by the Clergy, the Church would foon find great benefit, and God receive much glory by it, and the *Stray-Sheep* of our Countries, after

your

e

your Example, would return in Flocks t
her Folds.

Your *enquiring Genius*, and the Provi
dence of God led you to read fuch Book
and his Bleffing upon Reading of the
made you fee, and Correct your Errour
and though you have an advantage abov
moft others of the *Laity* in underftandin
Latin, yet there is already a great de
written in *English*, to let Pious, and I
quifitive Perfons into the knowledge
the Primitive Church, and Primitive Ch
ftianity, fuch as Dr. *Cave's* Primitive Ch
ftianity ; and his Learned, and elabor
Lives of the Fathers; *Fleury* of the Ma
ners, and Behaviour of the *Primitive Ch*
ftians, turned into *English* ; The Ecclef
ftical Hiftorians in a Noble new Editi
Illuftrated with Maps by the Learned
Welles; TheGenuine Epiftles of the Apof
lical Fathers by the Learned Bifhop *W*
from whom we wait for another Editi
The Learned Mr. *Bingham's Origines Ec*
fiaftica,or, *Antiquities of theChriftian Charl*
worthy to be read by all Men ; The
cond Part of the Clergy man's *Vade-Mec*
commended above ; Mr. *Reeves's* Apolo
of the Antient Chriftians, for which he w
deferves theThanks and Praife of all Lov
of Primitive Chriftianity, who cannot b
                                    deligl

delight to hear them speak in our Language the same things, with the same United Force of Wit and Reason, and with the same Charms of Eloquence that they did in their own. To these let me add the Exposition of the XXXIX. *Articles* by the late Bishop *Beveridge*, which the Learned World desires, and from which we may expect nothing but what is Primitive. There are other excellent Pens at Work in Books of the like nature with these, and I cannot but hope that God hath excited the Spirit of cultivating the more early *Ecclesiastical Antiquities*, in mercy to his Church. I could name * several other English Tracts upon several Subjects, full of Primitive Christian Divinity, were such a *Bibliotheca* fit for this Place. And besides those which are written in *English*, there are many excellent Pieces of the same kinds written in *French*, as *Du Pin's Nouvelle Bibliotheque des Auteurs Ecclesiastiques*, Translated into *English*; *Tillemont's Memoires, Pour Servir à l'histoire Ecclesiastique*, which also deserves to be Translated; the Works of St. *Cyprian* in *French*, which I cannot but wish that all Englishmen, who are not versed in *La-*

* *As the Principles of the Cyprianick Age, and the defence of it, &c.*

tin

The CONTENTS.

The Essay.

Propo.

The CONTENTS.

The CONTENTS.

III. *Who*

The CONTENTS.

The CONTENTS.

Epifcopacy

The CONTENTS.

The

The CONTENTS.

THE

A

Preliminary Discourse

OF

The various Opinions of the
Fathers concerning Rebaptization, and Invalid Baptisms,
with Remarks:

IN St *Cyprian*'s Days, about the middle
of the third Century, arose a great
Debate in the Church concerning the
Validity of Baptism administer'd by such
as were then either Hereticks or Schismaticks; St. *Cyprian* with the rest of the Bishops of the African Churches, together
with many of the Eastern Bishops, maintain'd, " That Catholick Bishops were oblig'd
" to Condemn all such Baptisms, and to hold
" them void and null, and by consequence
" not straight to *Confirm*, but first to Baptize
" all such, as having received no other than
" those False Baptisms, in those False, and
" Antichristian Communions, left them and
" came over to the One, True, Catholick,
" and only Salutary Communion.

B   " *Stephen*,

" *Stephen*, Bishop of *Rome*, and his Par-
" ty, maintain'd, That by the Evangelical
" Law, Catholick Bishops were bound to
" Ratify Heretical and Schismatical Bap-
" tisms, and to hold them Good and Valid;
" and to admit such as having been Bap-
" tiz'd by Hereticks, or Schismaticks, de-
" serted them, and came over to the True
" Catholick Communion, without giving
" them Catholick Baptism, or using any
" other Rite at their Reception, than that
" of Imposing the Hand for the Collation
" of the Holy Ghost.

" T H E *Stephanians* muster'd up a great
" many Arguments for the Validity of such
" Baptisms; They pleaded that Heretick
" themselves were not so nice, as to Bap
" tize those who came over from other He
" resies to their Communion : That all Ca-
" techumeni who died Unbaptized, wer.
" not therefore Damned; much less thos
" who had received Baptism, tho' from
" Hereticks, or Schismaticks : That to Re
" fuse those who were willing to forsak.
" Heresy or Schism, unless they would con-
" sent to be Re-baptized, was to obstruc.
" their coming over : That those who had
" been Baptized by *Philip* in *Samaria*, wer.
" not Re-baptized by the Apostles when
" they came among them (*Acts* 8.) and tha.
" they received Imposition of Hands only
" for the Collation of the Holy Ghost
" The'

" That tho' some in St. *Paul's* time Preached
" Christ out of Envy and Strife, *i. e.* from a
" Contentious and Schismatical Humour,
" yet he was pleased that Christ was Preach-
" ed : *(Phil* 1. 15.) That some Schismaticks,
" particularly the *Novatians,* observed the
" due Form, and propos'd the due Interro-
" gatories in Baptism : That the Efficacy of
" the Sacraments did not depend on the Or-
" thodoxy, or the Charity of the Admini-
" strators ; and that if Persons were Bap-
" tized in the Name of Christ, any manner
" of way, it was no matter who Baptized
" them : but the main Argument (as St.
" *Austin* afterwards reckon'd it) was that
" *Stephen,* Bishop of *Rome,* had had it hand-
" ed down to him by constant Tradition
" from St. *Peter* and St *Paul,* Founders of
" the Church of *Rome,* that those who cam
" over from Heretical or Schismatical Com-
" munions, to the Communion of the True
" Catholick Church should not be Re-bap-
" tized, and that all his Predecessors, Bi-
" shops of *Rome,* since the Days of those
" Apostles, had always conform'd their
" Practice to such unquestionable Tradition ;
" They had always Ratified, never Repudi-
" ated Heretical or Schismatical Baptisms.
    " THE Arguments of the *Cyprianists*
" against the Validity of such Baptisms were
" briefly these. St. *Cyprian* rejects the Bap-
" tisms of *Novatianus* upon this very Score

" that he was not a Bishop; *Cornelius* was
" the only true Bishop of *Rome*; no Valid
" Baptisms could be perform'd in that
" Church but by him, or in dependance on
" him: *Novatianus* disown'd all Depen-
" dance on him, separated from him, and
" pretended to be Bishop of *Rome* in oppo-
" sition to him; his Baptisms therefore
" could not be Valid; they could not be
" true Christian Sacraments, St. *Cyprian's*
" 69. Epist.   And in the same Epistle these
" three [To set up an Episcopal Chair] [To
" assume a Primacy] [and to pretend to a
" Sovereign or Independent Power of Bap-
" tizing and Offering, *i. e.* Consecrating
" the Holy Eucharist] he plainly makes
" Equivalent Phrases, and by them expres-
" ses the one Crime of *Novatianus* in stand-
" ing up as an Anti-Bishop to *Cornelius*:
" That all his Ministrations were of the same
" Kidney with those of *Corah, Dathan* and
" *Abiram*, which were wicked, damnable
" and naught, because perform'd in oppo-
" sition to the High Priest *Aaron*.   That it
" was unaccountable in **Bishops** to Ratify
" Heretical or Schismatical Baptisms; It
" was a Prostitution of the Honour both
" of the Catholick Church and the **Epis-**
" **copal College**: It tended to hinder Peo-
" ple from coming over from Heresy or
" Schism: It encourag'd them to think
" themselves safe and secure enough in
                              " either

" either ; for if there they had true Bap-
" tifm ; why not likewife a true Church
" and true Remiffion of Sins ? To weak-
" en the Authority of a pretended Cuftom
" to the contrary, he lays it down for an
" undoubted Truth, That we are not to
" be determin'd by any **Cuftoms** of that
" Nature, but to examine whether they
" will bear the Teft of Reafon. He affem-
" bled at *Carthage,* a Council of 71 Bifhops,
" who confirmed all that had been deter-
" min'd a little before in another Synod
" held in the fame City, concerning the
" Baptifm of Hereticks, *viz.* that it was
" null and void ; and about the fame time,
" immediately after this Council he writ
" a long Letter to *Jubaianus,* a Bifhop who
" had confulted him about this Queftion,
" wherein he urges abundance of Reafons
" and Texts of Scripture to fupport his
" own Opinion, and anfwer'd the Objecti-
" ons that were brought againft it. In ano-
" ther Letter to *Pompey* Bifhop of *Sabra,*
" he oppofes the **Truth** of the Gofpel, and
" the **firft Craditions** of the Apoftles both
" to the Cuftom and Tradition which *Ste-*
" *phen* had alledg'd for himfelf. *Firmilian*
" Bifhop of *Cefaria* in *Cappadocia,* in his
" Letter to St. *Cyprian,* openly condems the
" Procedure of *Stephen,* Bifhop of *Rome,*
" [who had anfwer'd St. *Cyprian* very rough-
" ly] extols St. *Cyprian's* Conduct, declares

himfelf

" himself entirely in favour of his Opinion,
" proves it by several Reasons ; and assures
" him it was the Ancient Custom of the A-
" siatick Churches ; and that it had been re-
" gulated many Years before in two Nume-
" rous Synods held at *Synnada* and *Iconium.*
" The same *Firmilian* Answers *Stephen*'s Plea
" of the constant Tradition he had handed
" down to him from St. *Peter* and St. *Paul,*
" as before mention'd ; That his, *viz.* Ste-
' phen's Allegation was utterly false ; he
" could have no such Tradition from those
" Apostles ; (*i. e.* St. *Peter* and St. *Paul,*)
" from whom he pretended to have it, and
" that for this very good Reason, that in
" their Days there were no Heretical Com-
" munions ; by consequence no Heretical
" Baptisms ; no Baptisms out of the true
" Communion of the Church Catholick,
" and that therefore he slander'd them by
' fathering such a Tradition on them, seeing
" it was certain that they taught the quite
' contrary in their Epistles : that St. *Paul*
" (*Acts* 19.) Re-baptized those who had
" been Baptized by *John the Baptist* ; ought
" not we then (says he) to *Baptize* those
" who come from Heresy to the Church ?
" Will any Man say that the Bishops now
" a days are greater than St. *Paul* was ?
" which they must needs be, if they are able
" to do that which he could not, if they
" by Imposition of Hands only, can give
                                    " the

" the Holy Ghoſt to Hereticks when they
" come to them. St. *Cyprian* in his Letter
" to *Jubaianus* Reaſons to this purpoſe a-
" gainſt the Validity of ſuch Baptiſms:
" 'Tis evident where and by whom the
" **Remiſſion of Sins** (which is given in
" baptiſm) can be given; for our Lord
" gave firſt to *Peter,* &c. that Power, that
" Whatſoever he ſhould looſe in Earth
" ſhould be looſed in Heaven; then after
" his Reſurrection he gave it to all the Apo-
" ſtles, when he ſaid (*John* 20. 21, 22, 23)
" *As my Father hath ſent me, &c.* Whence
" we learn that none have Authority to
" **Baptize** and **Remit Sins** but the **Bi-**
" **ſhops,** and thoſe who are founded in the
" Evangelical Law, and our Lords Inſtitu-
" tion, and that nothing can be bound or
" looſed *out of the Church,* ſeeing there is
" none *there* who has the Power of binding
" and looſing. Jeſus Chriſt (ſays *Fortuna-*
" *tus;* In the venerable Council of *Car-*
" *thage, Anno* 256) Our Lord and God,
" the Son of God the Father and Creator,
" built his Church upon a Rock, and not
" upon Hereſy; and he gave the Power of
" Baptizing to **Biſhops** and not to Hereticks.
" Thoſe therefore who are *out of the Church*
" and ſtand againſt Chriſt, and ſcatter his
" Flock, cannot Baptize, being *out of the*
" *Church.*

    I T would be endleſs to mention all the

Teſtimoines and Arguments, brought in that Age againſt the Validity of ſuch Baptiſms: I ſhall therefore name but one more, which ſeems to be of great moment for the Diſcovery of what was meant by Hereticks and Schiſmaticks in thoſe Days; and that is *Firmilian* who in one of his Letters ſays, " That he and all the Biſhops who met with " him in the Synod of *Iconium*, Decreed " that all thoſe ſhould be holden as Unbap- " tized, who were Baptized by ſuch as had " once been Biſhops in the Catholick Church, " if they were Baptized by them after they " had **Separated** from the Church : By which, and the other Monuments of that Age, it is evident, they held, that even Biſhops, and all other Lawful Miniſters loſt their **very Authority** to do any thing more in the Miniſterial Functions, when they either Schiſmatically or Heretically ſeparated themſelves from the Church of Chriſt : Hence doubtleſs it came to paſs that St. *Cyprian* and his Colleagues eſteem'd all their Ordinations null and void, and conſequently that the ſuppoſed Sacraments adminiſter'd by them, and thoſe whom they Ordain'd, were no true Chriſtian Sacraments, and therefore Invalid and Ineffectual : This, I ſay, appears to me to be the true Foundation of that great Diſpute concerning the Validity of Heretical and Schiſmatical Baptiſms, and which " St. *Cyprian* manag'd " with

" with fo much Chriftian Humility and Cha-
" rity, that tho *Stephen*, Bifhop of *Rome*,
" was fo far from agreeing to the Reafons
" of the Africans, (whether becaufe he
" imagin'd they had a defign to condemn
" the Roman Church, or becaufe he thought
" this Queftion was of too great Confe-
" quence) that he was enraged againft St.
" *Cyprian* and his Colleagues, and us'd their
" Leputies ill : Nay he prohibited all Chri-
" ftians belonging to his Church to receive
" or lodge them, depriving them, not only
" of Ecclefiaftical Communion, but alfo
" refufing them the common Civilities of
" Hofpitality; yet he [*i. e.* St. *Cyprian*]
" could not think of breaking Peace with
" them; of giving up Communion with
" them ; of Abftaining or Excommunicat-
" ing them.; Notwithftanding *Stephen* had
" taken upon him to Excommunicate thofe
" who oppos'd the Ratification of Heretical
" and Schifmatical Baptifms.   Upon the
" whole, the Perfecution of the Church
" by *Valerian*, *Anno* 257. put. an end to
" this Controverfy,   St. *Cyprian* **never** al-
" ter'd his Opinion ; the Greek Churches
" were for a long time after him divided up-
" on this Queftion ; the Council of *Arles*
" firft decided it in the Weft ; St *Auftin* fol-
" low'd its Decifion ; the Weftern Church
" has embrac'd this Opinion, *viz.* That
" Baptifm by Hereticks, in the Name of the
                              " Trinity,

" Trinity, is Valid ; and tho' the Eastern
" Churches have not agreed with her abso-
" lutely in this Point, yet they always made
" a Distinction between Hereticks, and dif-
" ferently receiv'd them.

" IN the 4th Century, St. *Athanasius* re-
" jects the Baptism of Hereticks. *Pacianus* says
" That Baptism Purifies from Sins, and Uncti-
" on brings down the Holy Spirit, *and both the*
" *One and the Other are applyed by the Hand*
" *and the Mouth of the Bishop.* Optatus, that
" the *Donatists* (who by the way were Schifmaticks) " committed a great Crime in
" reiterating Baptism, (*where 'tis to be noted*
that they Re-baptized the very Catholicks who
came over to them) " that 'tis not he who
" gives this Sacrament of Baptism that
" confers the Graces, but the Faith of him
" that receives it, and the Virtue of the
" Trinity. We ask (says he) if it be Law-
" ful to repeat Baptism given in the Name
" of the Trinity ? Ye maintain that it is
" Lawful ; We say that it is forbidden : The
" People are in suspence, *Let us therefore*
" *search after the Will of our Father, in the*
" *Gospel*, which will inform us that he who
" has been once Washed, needs not to be
" Washed again ; wherefore (adds he) We
" do not Re-baptize those who have been
" Baptized when they return again to us :
" He proves against the *Donatists*, that the
" Holiness of the Minister does not contri-
                                        " bute

" bute to the Validity of the Sacrament of
" Baptifm, and that becaufe the effect of
" the Sacrament is owing to God only,
" and in fhort, becaufe the Sacraments are
" Holy, and do Sanctify by themfelves:
" Yet he feems to think that we ought to
" Re-baptize thofe who were Baptized by
" Hereticks; but does not make the fame
" determination concerning thofe who were
" Baptized by Schifmaticks.

" St. *Bafil* maintains that the Antients
" were perfwaded that the Baptifm of He-
" reticks was **abfolutely** void: As for Schif-
" maticks he likes well enough, St. *Cyprian*
" and *Firmilian's* fubjecting them to the
" **fame Law**; becaufe being **feparate** from
" the Church, they had not the Holy
" Spirit, and fo could not give it; but,
" fays, he would not hinder the allowing
" of the Baptifms of Schifmaticks, fince
" the Bifhops of *Afia* had thought it con-
" venient to admit them: But tho the *En-*
" *cratites* were Schifmaticks, he declares
" that their Baptifm ought not to be ap-
" prov'd, and that thofe ought to be Re-
" baptized to whom they had given Bap-
" tifm; becaufe they gave it with Preci-
" pitation, on purpofe to **hinder** the re-
" ceiving of it from the Church; never-
" thelefs if the contrary Cuftom were Efta-
" blifhed he **confeffes it ought** to be fol-
" lowed.

" THE

" THE Council of *Eliberis*, *Anno* 305,
" Canon 38, declares, That a Chriftian
" who is neither Penitent, (*i. e.* not under
" Pennance,) nor a Bigamift, may Baptize
" in a Cafe of **Neceffity**, thofe who are
" on a Journey, being at a great diftance
" from a Church, upon Condition that he
" prefent him to the Bifhop, if he furvive,
" to be **perfected** by Impofition of Hands.

" THE Council of *Arles*, called by the
" Emperour, *Anno* 314, confifting of Thir-
" ty Three Weftern Bifhops. Canon 8. de-
" termines the famous **Queftion** about the
" Re-baptization of Hereticks, and Ordains
" concerning the Africans, who had **always**
" Re-baptiz'd them, that if any one leave
" a Herefy and return to the Church, he
" fhall be ask'd concerning the Creed, and
" if it be known that he was Baptiz'd in
" the Name of the Father, of the Son, and
" of the Holy Ghoft, Impofition of Hands
" only fhall be given him, that he may re-
" ceive the Holy Spirit ; but if he does not
" acknowledge the Trinity, I fuppofe 'tis
meant if while a Heretick he did not acknowledge the Trinity, or if the Heretick
who Baptiz'd him did not acknowledge
the Trinity, (the latter is the moft likely)
" he fhall be Re-baptiz'd.

BY the way, in this Canon ther is not
one Word about **Lay Baptifm** : And as
for the Hereticks who then Baptiz'd, they
had

had always, or at leaſt moſt commonly, received Ordination from the Hands of ſome
Catholick Biſhop or other; nay, generally the **Heretical Biſhops** were Conſecrated before they fell into Hereſy, by **Catholick
Biſhops**, or elſe afterwards by ſome Trick
or other, got private Conſecration from
them, that ſo their Hereſies might go down
the better with the People: And the ſame
we find concerning Schiſmaticks in thoſe
Days.

THE Council of *Neocæſarea*, *Anno* 314,
Canon 1. ſays, " That if a Prieſt Marries
" after he has been Ordain'd, he ought to
" be degraded. How conformable this Canon is to the Goſpel of Chriſt, let all ſeri-
ous Chriſtians Obſerve and Conſider; I
mention it therefore, only to ſhew, that in
thoſe Days Councils were not Infallible in
all their Decrees.

THE Council of *Nice*, *Anno* 325, con-
ſiſting of about 300 Biſhops, Canon 19.
Ordains, " That the *Paulianiſts* ſhall be
" Re-baptiz'd who return to the Church.
In this Council alſo a Canon was propos'd
for obliging Biſhops, Prieſts, and Deacons
to obſerve **Celibacy**.

" IN the Council of *Carthage*, *Anno*
" 348, before they proceeded to make Ca-
" nons, the Preſident advis'd thus: we muſt
" have ſuch regard to this time of Peace,
" that we neither weaken the Obligation
" of

" of the Laws, nor yet Prejudice the pre-
" sent Unity by **too much Severity**.
" Then the first Head propos'd was about
" Re-baptization; he ask'd whether that
" Man ought to be Re-baptiz'd who at his
" Baptism made profession of believing the
" Trinity. The **Bishops** answered, God
" forbid; We declare that this Re-bapti-
" zation is Unlawful, contrary to the Or-
" thodox Faith, and the Ecclesiastical Dif-
" cipline

THE Council of *Laodicea* between *An-*
no 360 and 370, Canon 8, says, " That
" they must be wholly Baptized anew, who
" come from the Sect of the *Montanists.*

THE third Council of *Constantinople,*
Anno 383, in the last Canon, concerning
the manner of receiving Hereticks, who
offer themselves to return into the Bosom
of the Church, it is Ordain'd, " That the
" *Arians, Macedonians, Sabbatians, Nova-*
" *tians, Quarto decimani, Tetratites* and *A-*
" *pollinarists*, shall be receiv'd, after they
" have made profession of their Faith, and
" anathematiz'd their Errours, by the Un-
" ction of the Holy Spirit, and the Chrifm
" wherewith they shall be Anointed on the
" Forehead, the Eyes, the Hands, the Mouth,
" the Ears, at the pronouncing of these
" Words, *This is the Seal of the Holy Spi-*
" *rit :* as to the *Eunomians,* the *Montanists,*
" the *Sabellians,* and all the other Here-
                                    " ticks,

" ticks, the Council Ordains that they shall
" be receiv'd like Pagans, *&c.* and at last
" they shall be Baptiz'd.

" THE Council of *Capua, Anno* 390,
" declar'd that it was not Lawful to use
" Rebaptization, **Re-ordination**, and the
" **Translation** of **Bishops**

THE second Council of *Carthage, Anno*
390, in the second Canon renews the Law
Established in the preceeding Council concerning the *Celibacy* of Bishops, Priests and
Deacons. The 8th Canon declares, " That
" if a Priest Excommunicated by his own
" Bishop undertake to offer up the Sacrifi-
" ces in Private, and to set up **Altar** against
" **Altar**, thereby making a **Schism**, he
" ought to be anathematiz'd; because there
" is but **One Church One Faith** and
" **One Baptism.** My Remark on this
Canon is, That this **One Baptism** can-
not be suppos'd to be out of this **One
Church**, and therefore is only in it.

THE third Council of *Carthage, Anno*
398, Canon 100, says, " That a Woman
" ought not to take upon her to Baptize.

" THE Council of *Carthage, Anno* 401,
" second Session, orders bishops, Priests,
" and Deacons to have no more to do with
" their **Wives**, *Directly contrary to the*
" *Law of God.*

" In the 5th Century flourish'd St. *Au-*
" *gustin,* Bishop of *Hipo* in *Africa*; he ar-
" gued

" gued vigorously against the *Donatists* who
" began their 𝕾𝖈𝖍𝖎𝖘𝖒 by a separation of
" some Af.ican Bithops, and proceeded so
" far as to reckon all other Churches as un-
" clean, and indeed to be no Churches at
" all, and consequently when any Catho-
" lick came over to their Party, they would
" not admit him without Re-baptization,
" making use of St *Cyprian* and his Col-
" leagues Authority, who taught, " That
" Baptism administer'd by Hereticks and
" Schismaticks could not be Valid because
" they were out of the Church, and the
" *Donatists* esteem'd the Catholicks to be
" no better than such.

" St. *Augustin* in Opposition to them,
" undertakes to prove that tho' his Party
" were not the Church, yet the *Donatists*
" were not to Baptize them a second time;
" he confesses that Baptism perform'd with-
" out naming the 𝕿𝖗𝖎𝖓𝖎𝖙𝖞 is Null; but
" affirms, That if it be administred in the
" Name of the 𝕿𝖗𝖎𝖓𝖎𝖙𝖞 it is Valid, 𝖜𝖍𝖔𝖘𝖔
" 𝖊𝖛𝖊𝖗 he be that Administers it, and ought
" not to be repeated; That neither the
" Ministers 𝕱𝖆𝖎𝖙𝖍 as to Religion, nor his
" Sanctity avail any thing to the Validity
" of Baptism; That it is God and not the
" Minister who gives the Holy Spirit and
" worketh the Remission of Sins.

BUT here, before I proceed further, I
must observe, that it does not hence follow

low, that becauſe the Faith or Sanctity of the Miniſter avails nothing to the Validity of Baptiſm, therefore his 𝕬𝖚𝖙𝖍𝖔𝖗𝖎𝖙𝖞 by which he acts avails nothing thereto ; for 𝕬𝖚𝖙𝖍𝖔𝖗𝖎𝖙𝖞 may very well be, and often is, 𝕯𝖎𝖘𝖙𝖎𝖓𝖈𝖙 and 𝕾𝖊𝖕𝖆𝖗𝖆𝖙𝖊 from both thoſe excellent Qualities : And again, every one will grant that it is *God* and not the *Miniſter* who gives the Holy Spirit, *&c.* What then, does it thence follow that any Perſon may Adminiſter ? Can it be reaſonably expected that God ſhould concur with the 𝖀𝖘𝖚𝖗𝖕𝖆𝖙𝖎𝖔𝖓𝖘 of thoſe who Act herein without 𝖍𝖎𝖘 𝕮𝖔𝖒𝖒𝖎𝖘𝖘𝖎𝖔𝖓, nay and in 𝖔𝖕𝖕𝖔𝖘𝖎𝖙𝖎𝖔𝖓 thereto, [as is the Caſe with us.] Certainly no ; it cannot : For however he may Diſpenſe with the 𝖜𝖆𝖓𝖙 of a Sacrament, yet he has no where promis'd to give 𝕰𝖋𝖋𝖎𝖈𝖆𝖈𝖞 to thoſe Adminiſtrations which are in any reſpect Contrary to his own Inſtitutions ; and to me it ſeems a meer Fool-hardineſs and Preſumption to expect it.

But to proceed :

St. *Auguſtin* in the 7th Book of Baptiſm, Cap. 53. ſays thus, " It is asked " whether that Baptiſm is to be approved " which is Adminiſter'd by an Unbap-

C   tized

" tized Perfon, who out of Curiofity
" has learned the way of Baptizing among
" Chriftians ? it is asked further, whether
" it be neceffary for the Validity of Bap-
" tifm, that he who either Adminifters
" or Receives it be Sincere ? And if they
" fhould be only in Jeft, whether their
" Baptifm ought to be Adminifter'd again
" in the Church ? Whether Baptifm Con-
" ferr'd in Derifion, as that would be
" which fhould be Adminifter'd by a Co-
" median, might be accounted Valid ?
" Whether Baptifm Adminifter'd by an
" Actor, may become Valid, when he that
" receives it is well difpos'd ?

HE Anfwers to thefe, and fuch like
Queftions, " That the fecureft way is to
" return no Anfwer to Queftions that ne-
" ver were decided in any Council Gene-
" ral or National ; but he adds, fhould
" any Man meeting with me at fuch Coun-
" cil, ask my Advice about thefe Quefti-
" ons, and that it were my turn to declare
" my Opinion, having not heard other
" Mens Opinions, which I might prefer
" before my own, &c. I fhould without
" difficulty acknowledge, That they all
" receive Baptifm truly, in any Place
" whatfoever, and by whomfoever Ad-
" minifter'd, if on their Part they receive

" it with Faith and Sincerity. I am apt
" also to believe that such as receive Bap-
" tism in the Church, or in what is sup-
" posed to be the Church, are truely Bap-
" tiz'd, as to the Sacramental part of the
" Action, whatsoever be their Intention :
" But as for Baptism Administer'd and re-
" ceived *out of the Church*, in Raillery,
" Contempt, and to make Sport, I could
" not approve the same without a Reve-
" lation.

HE endeavours to overthrow the Reasons and Testimonies of the *Cyprianists*
against the Validity of Heretical and Schismatical Baptisms by the Comparison *of
conceal'd Hereticks* and *evil Ministers*, with
known Hereticks and *Schismaticks*, " for
" (says he) if the Baptism Administred
" by the former is Valid and not to be
" renewed, why should not the same thing
" be said of the Latter, since all the
" Reasons that are alledg'd for the Nullity
" of the Baptism of Hereticks, may also
" belong to *evil Ministers?* It is said for
" Example, *That to give the Holy Ghost
" one must have it, that Hereticks have it
" not; and consequently that they cannot
" give it :* Why may we not Reason af-
" ter the same manner, concerning Bap-
" tism conferr'd by Conceal'd Herericks

" or

" or by Wicked Priests? Have they the
" Holy Ghost to give? Thus St *Augustin.*

I cannot but take notice here, that this
Great Man does not appear (to me) to
have made the Comparison according to
the design of St. *Cyprian,* and his Colleagues; for by the manner of handling
this Dispute in those Days, 'tis plain to
me that the Hereticks and Schismaticks
were suppos'd to be **Excommunicate,**
and consequently to have lost all Valid
Power and Authority for the Administration of Christian Sacraments, being themselves *out of the Church*; whereas the *Conceal'd Heretick* and *Evil Minister* not having separated themselves from, nor been
excluded out of the Church, cannot, during this their Secrecy, loose that **Visible
Authority** wherewith they were at first
invested, and we have no **other** Authority
to trust to, except we had the Gift of dis-
cerning Spirits; so that the Reasons a-
gainst the Validity of Baptism Administer'd by **known** Excommunicated Hereticks, and Schismaticks, will not equally
hold good against the Validity of Baptism
conferr'd by **unknown** Hereticks and Evil
Priests, who still continue in *External
Communion* with the **Church**; because
the

the former have not, but the latter have that **visible Authority** and **Commission** which Christ gave them to Administer his Sacraments ; as is plain from the Example of *Judas Iscariot*, whom our Saviour vested with the Divine Commission, notwithstanding his great Wickedness.

Leo, Bishop of *Rome*, in his 18th Answer to several Questions put to him by *Rusticus*, Bishop of *Narbonne*, *Anno* 442, says, " That it is sufficient to lay hands " upon, and call upon the Holy Spirit, " over those that do remember that they " have been Baptiz'd, but know not in " what Sect.

Gennadius, a Priest of *Marseille*, affirms, " That there is **But One Baptism**, and " that we must not Baptize them again " who have been Baptized by Hereticks, " with the Invocation of the Name of the " Trinity ; but they who have not been " Baptiz'd in the Name of the Trinity, " ought to be Rebaptized, because such " a Baptism is not True.

THE 2d Council of *Arles*, Canon 2. says, " That no Man may be made a " Priest who is Married, unless they will " renounce the use of Marriage, which " they call by the Name of Conversi- " on.

" Canon

" Canon 17. The *Bonosiaci*, who Bap-
" tize as well as the *Arians* in the Name
" of the Trinity ; it is sufficient to ad-
" mit them into the Church, by Chrism,
" and Imposition of Hands.

St. *Gregory* about the latter end of the
6th Century, speaking about the return of
several sorts of Hereticks into the Church,
says, " That they are Baptized when they
" re-enter into the Church, the Baptism
" which they have received not being
" true, since it was not given in the Name
" of the Trinity.   When it is uncertain
" whether a Person has been Baptized or
" Confirmed, we must Baptize or Confirm
" them rather than suffer them to perish
" in this Doubt.

Gregory II. a little after, *Anno* 700, in
his Decretal Epistle, answering several
Questions put to him by *Boniface*, Article
3. " forbids to Re-baptize those who have
" been once Baptized in the Name of the
" Trinity, altho it were by *a wicked*
" *Priest.*

" *Gregory* III. Orders that they shall be
" Baptized again in the Name of the
" Trinity, who have been Baptized by
" Heathens.   And also that those shall
' be Re-baptized, who have been Bap-
' tized by a Priest that hath Sacrificed to
" *Jupiter*

" *Jupiter,* or eaten Meat offer'd to Idols.
Thus far I think may fuffice to have Col-
lected what has been faid about Re-baptization. Becaufe

IT is well known that the Church began to be miferably over-run with 𝕰𝖗𝖗𝖔𝖚𝖗
and 𝕾𝖚𝖕𝖊𝖗𝖋𝖙𝖎𝖙𝖎𝖔𝖓 after the Year of Chrift
300, and that many Decrees of Councils and Fathers were from that time
founded, not upon the Reveal'd Will of
God in his Written Word, but upon pretended *Traditions,* and a *Difpenfing Power*
affum'd by fome of the *Governours* of the
Church, witnefs thofe Decrees which require Celibacy in the Clergy, *&c.* as
you may fee in feveral of the above cited Councils, for which Reafon I might
very well have fpared my Labour of making many of thefe Collections; but becaufe
I have been told that it becomes me to
reft fatisfied in the *Determinations* of the
Chriftian Church about this matter, I
thought it not amifs to enquire into them
thus far; to the intent, that I might fee
whether I could procure any 𝖜𝖊𝖑𝖑-𝖌𝖗𝖔𝖚𝖓𝖉-
𝖊𝖉 Satisfaction from their *Authority;* and
indeed I muft acknowledge, that if this
had been a Thing *Indifferent* in its own
Nature, and not 𝖉𝖊𝖙𝖊𝖗𝖒𝖎𝖓𝖊𝖉 by the *word*
of God, but left to the Wifdom and Pru-

C 4   dence

dence of the Church to Decree as she should think convenient and necessary, I ought to have acquiesc'd with *such Determinations*, but the Case stands otherwise with me, I esteem Baptism in all its Essential Parts to be a **fundamental** of Christianity, (as the Apostle himself has told us,) a *Positive Institution* made by God himself ; and the Holy Scriptures are **clear enough** for the Determination of all the Necessaries thereof, as well as of all other Fundamental Points of our Religion, and therefore the Decrees of Fathers and Councils have no more weight with me in this matter, than what they receive from their Conformity to those Divine Oracles, which are the only Rule of our Faith and Practice in Fundamentals, as all *sound Protestants* have affirm'd.

BESIDES, the Councils of *Carthage*, *Iconium* and *Synnada*, together with the Customs of the Asiatick and African Churches, confirming St. *Cyprian's* Doctrine, have as much (if not more) Authority to sway my Judgment in this matter, as the Council of *Arles* and the after Determinations of other Councils and Fathers ; for these latter can pretend to no more Divine Authority than the former.

I

I am very well satisfied. that ther is but **One true Christian Baptism** which ought not to be repeated upon those who have receiv'd it: I find my self under an Impossibility to believe, that this **One Baptism** is any other, than what Christ himself Instituted just before his Ascension into Heaven ; I reckon an Essential Part of this Institution (and I humbly hope in the sequel of this Discourse to prove it) to be the **Divine Authority** of the **Administrator** as well as the Water, and the Form of Administration.

I cannot be satisfied, that the Person who is said to have Baptiz'd me ever had this Authority, nay I know to the contrary, and also that he was actually in *opposition* to it ; and tho' his meaning were never so good, yet I cannot think God concurr'd with such an Usurpation, when it was done without *Any Necessity at all in a Christian Country, where truly Authoriz'd Ministers might have been had with as much, if not greater ease and speed than he ;* for which Reasons I find no solid Foundation for believing that I have received this **One Baptism**, especially since I my self should with great Reason have refus'd that which he Administer'd, if I had been put to my own free Choice, as it's
certain

certain I could not then, being but an Infant. I doubt not but some will say, *That I need not concern my self so much about that which I had no hand in, and wherein I was wholly Passive;* if ther was any Fault in such my Baptism, 'twas none of mine, but theirs who had the Care of me : To whom I return this short Answer, That the Parent's or Godfather's and Godmother's Act and Deed is *interpretatively* the Child's, and he must make it *really* his own when he comes to Years, by taking it upon himself; so that if **then** he owns their Sinful Act (knowing it to be such) he makes himself **partaker** with them in the Sin.

BUT to return to the Dispute in St. *Cyprian*'s time, and the Decrees then and since made about it; I cannot Dissemble my Thoughts that the Arguments and Determinations against his Doctrine and Practice, have nothing of that Reason and Solidity which an Inquisitive Person might justly expect in them : And that on the contrary, St. *Cyprian* and his Colleagues defend their Assertion [*that the Baptisms of* Hereticks *and* Schismaticks *are Invalid*] with so much Judgment and Cogency of Argument, (*founded upon the Topick of such* Hereticks *and* Schismaticks, *being destitute*

of

of Holy Orders while they were out of the Church of Chriſt) that I wonder how it could poſſibly have come to paſs, that their Doctrine ſhould be afterwards exploded ; eſpecially when I conſider that what they taught and practic'd herein, was confirmed by **numerous Councils** in thoſe *earlier Days,* wherein Truth was more prevalent than afterwards ; and *Tertullian* long before affirm'd the ſame thing, " *That Baptiſm is reſerv'd to the Biſhop ;* " Hereticks are not able to give it, be- " cauſe they have it not, and therefore it " is that we have a **Rule** to Re-baptize " them. And to go ſtill further backward to the Days wherein ſome of the Apoſtles might be ſtill living ; St. *Ignatius,* a Glorious Martyr, and Biſhop of *Antioch, Anno Dom.* 71. in his Epiſtle to the *Smyrneans,* ſays, " Let that **Sacrament** be judg'd " *effectual and firm,* which is diſpens'd by " the **Biſhop**, or him to whom the Biſhop " has committed it. It is not **Lawful** " without the Biſhop either to Baptize or " Celebrate the Offices : But what he ap- " proves of, according to the good plea- " ſure of God, that is **firm** and **Safe** " and ſo we do every thing **Securely**.

THIS is ſo exactly agreeable to St. *Cyprian*'s Doctrine, that 'tis no wonder he

he adher'd to it all the Days of his Life;
and it seems to me, that nothing could
have given *Credit* and *Reputation* to the
contrary Opinion, but the *monstrous* en-
crease of 𝔥𝔢𝔯𝔢𝔰𝔶 and 𝔖𝔠𝔥𝔦𝔰𝔪 afterwards,
which brought in abundance of Damnable Doctrines, and Practices [*two of which
you may see in the preceeding Collections*]
infomuch, that at laft ther was but little
of Solid and Substantial Religion to be
found in the World.

AND now, after all that has been
faid, I declare that it is not my Defign to
meddle with the Cyprianick Difpute in
this Difcourfe; my bufinefs is not to enquire whether thofe who were *once duly
Authoriz'd*, and afterwards fall into 𝔥𝔢𝔯𝔢𝔰𝔶 or 𝔖𝔠𝔥𝔦𝔰𝔪, and thereby feparate themfelves, or are excluded from the Church,
can adminifter Valid Sacraments and Ordinations during this their Separation:
no, I fhall not fo much as touch upon
this at all, becaufe I don't think my Cafe
affected by it; all that I need concern my
felf about, is, whether thofe who act in
oppofition to the acknowledg'd and *duly
Authoriz'd* Minifters of Chrift; and who
themfelves were 𝔫𝔢𝔳𝔢𝔯 duly Authoriz'd,
can Adminifter *truly Valid Baptifm*, and
whether the Receivers of *thofe Baptifms*

                                        can

can safely rest satisfied with them, especially when they know of this want of Power and Authority in the Administrator. This is my Case, and this is all that I concern my self about.

AND therefore I wrote the following ESSAY in a Mathematical Method of *Definition, Axiom,* and *Proposition,* for the Information of my own Judgment, in this great Affair : it was not at first design'd for publick view, but finding others have been, and it may be still do Labour under the same Circumstances with my self, I thought it might not be unacceptable to them ; and if they shall reap any benefit thereby, or if some abler Pen will undertake to mend my Faults, by letting the World see something *more Correct* and *exact* for that *purpose,* (The *only* Motive of my Writing) I shall obtain my end, which God be praised is not mixt with any alloy of worldly Gain, or desire of Humane Applause for this Undertaking.

AS for *Caviling* and *Disputing* 'tis not my design to concern my self (and loose my Precious time) in such *endless impertinencies :* If any one will *candidly* shew me my *Errours,* I shall heartily thank him for so doing ; but I declare before-hand, that no less than such *Demonstration* as the Nature

ture of the Thing will bear, can ever go
down with me for Conviction ; I am not
to be put off with the Authority of any
great Names, *Separate* from *Scripture and
Reason*, for this has caus'd too much *Errour* in the World already, and 'tis high
time now to reform from it.

London, February, 28. 1708.

Lay

THE
INTRODUCTION.

Of the Nature and Obligation of Divine Poſitive Inſtitutions of Religion.

Definitions.

I. A *Divine Poſitive Inſtitution* of Religion is, that which God himſelf requires and commands to be done, and which (*having no intrinſick or moral excellency in it ſelf*) without his Command and Appointment we could never have been bound to the Obſervance of; nor ever have convey'd to us by the Obſervation thereof, any **Supernatural** Benefit or Advantage whatſoever.

II. THE

II. THE *Essential Parts* of a Divine Positive Institution, are those which we are oblig'd constantly to observe, as long as the *utmost duration*, of the Force and Obligation of the Institution it self.

III. I call an Act *Invalid* for the purposes of such an Institution, when we have *no just Reason* to expect, that God should so far concur with that Act, as to *convey* by means thereof, *those supernatural Advantages* he has annex'd to the Institution.

IV. BY the *Supernatural Advantages* Annex'd to an Institution, I mean all those *Spiritual Priviledges* and *Benefits* which by Nature we cannot have, and which God has promis'd to bestow, upon *Condition* of our *duly* Performing that Institution, which he has made to be the *Ordinary means* of Conveying those Benefits to us.

V. By the *Divine Authority* of the Administrator, I mean *that Commission* which God at first gave to Men, and which they have ever since handed down to others, by his Order and Appointment, to Administer in his Holy Ordinances.

AXIOM'S

AXIOMS
OR,
Undeniable Maxims.

I. THE *Effential Parts* of any thing, are of the fame Nature as the *whole.*

II. GOD himfelf may *difpenfe* with any of his own Pofitive Inftitutions, either in whole or in Part; and beftow the Benefits annex'd to them, when, to whom, and how he pleafes.

III. *NO Ecclefiaftical* or *Civil Authority* can Difpenfe with any Divine Pofitive Inftitution, either in whole, or in any Effential Part, fo long as it is binding and obliging to us.

IV. THE *only way* to determine whether an Act is Valid or Invalid, for the purpofes of a Divine Pofitive Inftitution, is, to know whether that Act be *Lawful* or *Unlawful*, Agreeable, or Contrary to the Will of God, which is to be found *no where*, but either in the Inftitution it felf, or in fome other Part or Parts of his Writ-

D ten.

ten Word, *relating* to the *same Inftitution.*

V. NO Power or Authority on Earth,
can by any after Act (*not appointed by God
for that purpofe,*) make that which before
was Invalid, to become as Valid as Conforming to the Divine Inftitution it felf
would have made it.

VI. He that *knows* to do good, and
does it not, to *him* it is *Sin*; and a *Con-
tinnance* in Sin, can bring *no Supernatural*
Benefit or Advantage.

PROPOSITION I.

EVERY Effential Part of a Divine
Pofitive Inftitution of Religion, is of E-
qual Obligation and Neceffity to us.

DEMONSTRATION. This is evident,

FIRST, from the very Nature of fuch
an Inftitution, which (by *Definition* 1.)
has no *intrinfick excellency,* or moral Virtue

tue to oblige us to obferve it, till the Divine Command lays that neceffity upon us : fo that now we are oblig'd *only* by Virtue of the *Authority Commanding* ; which being but *One, (i. e.* That of God) muft neceffarily reach to *every Effential Part* of the Inftitution, and thereby make them all of equal Authority and equally neceffary and obliging to us ; becaufe *they are every one* of the fame Nature as the Inftitution it felf, (*by Axiom* 1.) And

Secondly, this is further evident (*from Definition* 2.) fince we are *conftantly* bound to obferve every fuch *Effential Part* as long as the Inftitution it felf fhall have any Force or Virtue. Therefore fince every one of thefe Parts have but *one Authority,* without any *Inherent* Virtue feparate therefrom ; and are alfo binding as long as the Inftitution fhall laft ; it muft needs be certain, that they are *all of equal Obligation and Neceffity* to us But this is fo very plain at the firft Propofal to all Intelligent Perfons, that it hardly deferves the Name of a Propofition to be Demonftrated, and therefore I fhall not loofe more time about it

D 2   COROL.

COROLLARY.

HENCE it follows, that as no Human Authority can difpenfe with any Divine Pofitive Inftitution ; (*Axiom* 3.) fo neither can they give any *Superiority* of excellency, or neceffity to one Effential Part thereof more than to another, becaufe, they are all equally neceffary and obliging; and have their whole *Force* and *Energy* merely from the Divine Command.

PROPOSITION II.

WHOSOEVER juftly efteems an Act (*said to be done in purfuance of a Divine Pofitive Inftitution*) to be *wholly* Null and Invalid for want of one Effential Part of that Inftitution, ought alfo to *acknowledge* that fuch an Act is as *much* Null and Void when it wants *but any other One Effential Part* of the fame Inftitution.

DEMON. For he can *reafonably* judge that Act to be Invalid, only becaufe it is unlawful, or contrary to the Inftitution ; (*Axiom* 4.) So that, the *want* of that Effential Part being unlawful, he thence concludes the Invalidity of the Act : Now,
forafmuch

forafmuch as all the Effential Parts of the Inftitution are of *equal* Authority and Neceffity to us (*by the foregoing Propofition*) it muft neceffarily follow, that the *Omiffion* of any one of them will be. *equally Unlawful* or Invalid ; and confequently fuch a Deficient Act, as wants any one of thofe Effential Parts, being by him juftly efteem'd Invalid, ought alfo for the *fame Reafon* to be efteemed as much Invalid when he knows it to want *but any other One Effential Part* of the fame Inftitution, which was the thing to be prov'd.

COROLLARY.

HENCE it unavoidably follows, that ther can be *no fuch thing* as a *Partial Invalidity* through the Omiffion of any Effential Part of a Divine Pofitive Inftitution; for if the Act be *wholly Null* for want of one fuch Part, it muft be alfo *entirely void* for the want of any other ; by Reafon of the *equal Authority and Neceffity* of every Effential Part.

PROPOSITION. III.

HE who knows himfelf bound to Conform to a Divine Pofitive Inftitution *in all its Effential Parts*, and is convinc'd

that

that he has not fo far conform'd; can have no juft Grounds to expect the *Supernatural Benefits* annex'd to that Inftitution, till he has done his utmoft for the obtaining of them, by endeavouring an *entire Conformity* to every Effential Part of the faid Inftitution.

DEMON. This wants but little Proof; For thus entirely to obey the Inftitution is certainly good; and he who knows this and does it not, to him it is Sin (*Axiom* 6.) which if he continues in, no Supernatural Advantage can accrue to him thereby (*by the fame Axiom*) much lefs thofe Benefits annex'd to the obfervance of the Inftitution; and confequently he ought to do his utmoft for the obtaining of them by endeavouring, *&c.* as was to be Demonftrated.

AN

AN
ESSAY

To prove the

Invalidity of Lay Baptism;

Eſpecially to thoſe who know
that 'twas Adminiſter'd to them,

By one in oppoſition to

The Divine Right
OF THE

Apoſtolical Succeſſion.

CHRISTIAN *Baptiſm*, is, a Divine
Poſitive Inſtitution of our moſt Holy Religion, whereby 'tis appoint-
ed, that the **Apoſtles** and their **Succeſſors**
to the *End of the World,* ſhould [*by Virtue
of a Particular Commiſſion which Chriſt gave
them for this purpoſe*] either themſelves in
Perſon, or by **their Subſtitutes,** enter

D 4　　　　　　　　　into

into Difciplefhip, or into the Church of
Chrift, All Nations, Baptizing them *In the
Name* of the Father, and of the Son, and
of the Holy Ghoft, *&c.* The *Supernatural Priviledges* and Benefits Annex'd to
this Inftitution, are, the Pardon of Sins,
The Gift of the Holy Ghoft, and Eternal
Life after Death ; or as the Church of
England words it, " *Being by Nature born*
" *in Sin and the Children of Wrath, we are*
" *hereby made the Children of Grace ; Mem-*
" *bers of Chrift ; Children of God, and In-*
" *heritors (or Heirs) of the Kingdom of*
" *Heaven* : which vaft and unfpeakable Advantages none can *ordinarily* have any
Right or Title to, but thofe who are *duly*
admitted to them by this *One True Chriftian Baptifm.*

THAT it is a *Pofitive Inftitution* is certain from hence ; that before the Divine
Command enjoyn'd it we were never
bound to obferve it, either in whole or in
part ; wafhing us *then* with *Water,* had no
intrinfick or moral Virtue to give us any
Spiritual Advantages, nor would it have
had any thing more of *efficacy* for that
purpofe if we had been Wafh'd with Water,
and at the fame time ufed the Words *In the
Name of the Father, and of the Son and of
the Holy Ghoft ;* for thefe Words being
pro-

pronounc'd could *then* have had no more
Virtue than others: neither would it have
ſignified any thing to us whether we had
been Waſh'd either by our *ſelves alone,* or
by ſome *other Perſon*; or whether that other
Perſon were a Common Man, or one *ſet
apart* by Conſent of the *People* for that
end. None of theſe Things could by any
excellency in their own Nature have convey'd to us any *Spiritual Benefits* whatſoever, nor could we have been oblig'd in
a Religious Senſe to obſerve *any one* of
them; becauſe the Divine Command had
not enjoyn'd them; this I ſuppoſe all will
acknowledge, and conſequently that our
Obligation to receive *Chriſtian Baptiſm,*
and *from them* by whom it is order'd to be
Adminiſter'd, is *wholly* founded upon the
divine Command on which *alone* depends
the whole Force and Energy of a Divine
Poſitive Inſtitution of Religion (according to *definition* 1.) and that therefore the
Adminiſtration of *Chriſtian Baptiſm in all
its Parts,* is no other than a *mere Poſitive
Inſtitution,* exactly agreeable to the ſaid
Definition. This being premis'd, I proceed
now to Demonſtrate what are the Eſſential Parts of this great Inſtitution of Chri-
ſtianity, *on the Part of the Adminiſtration
thereof.*

PRO-

PROPOSITION I.

THAT *on the Part of the Administra-tion*, The Divine Authority of the *Administrator*; The matter [*Water*] and the *Form* of Administring, [*In the Name of the Father, and of the Son, and of the Holy Ghost*] are every one of them *Essential Parts* of the Divine Positive Institution of Christian Baptism.

DEMON. That the *Water*, and the *Form* of Administration in the *Name* of the *Trinity*, are Essential Parts of this Institution, was never Disputed by any but Hereticks, and even these *(except such as the* Quakers*)* never oppos'd against the *Water's* being so; but only against the Form of Administration in the Name of the Trinity. I shall not make it my business to endeavour their Conviction, who oppose the plain and express words of the Institution, and from whence *All Sound and Orthodox* Christians have unanimously agreed, to pronounce Baptism Null and Void, when Administer'd without expressing the Names of all the *three Sacred Persons*; because such Baptisms are directly against the Institution it self.

TAKING

TAKING it therefore for granted by all, who have any value for this Holy Ordinance, that the *Water* and the *Form* of Adminiftration in the Name of the Trinity, are Effential Parts thereof; I fhall fpend no time about the Proof of it; but proceed to Demonftrate, that the *Divine Authority* of the *Adminiftrator*, is alfo an Effential Part of the fame Inftitution; or (which is the fame thing) that the *Divine Authority of the Adminiftrator*, is to be *conftantly* obferv'd by us, *as long* as the *utmoft Duration* of the Force and Obligation of the Divine Pofitive Inftitution of *Chriftian Baptifm*, And, that it is fo, will be evident,

1. From the General Confideration of God's making the *Divine Authority of the Adminiftrator*, to be an *Effential Part* of his own Pofitive Inftitutions under the *Mofaic* Law,

2. By the *Example* of our Saviour's not taking upon him to Minifter in fuch Holy things, till he was *particularly* and *externally Commiffion'd* for that purpofe.

3. From the Words of Inftitution of Chriftian Baptifm.

4. From

4. From the Defign and Benefits thereof.

5. From the conftant Practice of thofe
who *truly are*, and of others who pretend
to be the *Lawful Minifters* of the Chriftian Church.

6. From the *Doctrine* and *Practice* of
the *Church of* England in particular.

Firft, I fay the General Confideration
of God's making the Divine Authority
of the Adminiftrator, to be an Effential
Part of his own Pofitive Inftitutions under the Mofaic Law, will go a great way
towards proving the like under the Gofpel
Difpenfation ; becaufe, the things that were
then written, were not written for their
fakes *only*, but alfo for our Example (as
the Apoftle has told us) and as he has
moft excellently argued, almoft throughout
his whole Epiftle to the *Hebrews*, wherein he makes the Comparifon between the
Mofaic-Law, and the *Gofpel*, and gives a
vaft *preference* to the *Latter* before the former.   'Tis therefore worthy our Confideration that in the Law, *none* could ap-
proach the Divine Prefence in the *Adminiftration* of his Pofitive Inftitutes, but
                                    thofe

thofe who were firft *Authoriz'd* by *him* for
that purpofe ; and therefore we find that
when *Corah, Dathan,* and *Abiram,* exceed-
ed their own bounds no farther, than the
Offering of Incenfe, ther was no lefs than
a Miracle wrought, the very Earth was
made to open its Mouth and fwallow them,
their Wives and their Children, and all
that they had ; and a Fire from the Lord
confum'd two hundred and fifty Princes,
Accomplices with 'em in the fame Crime ;
to make them a ftanding *Example* to future
Ages, that none might Ufurp the Authority of Adminiftring in his Pofitive Inftitutions without a *Commiffion* firft receiv'd
from him. Nay, fo Jealous was God of
this Honour, that he fuddenly ftruck *Uzza*
dead, only for putting forth his Hand to
fave the Ark (as he thought) from falling
when it was fhook ; *his Zeal* was no defence for him, God would not pardon
but punifh him for it, becaufe 'twas none
of his *Bufinefs* to meddle in fuch Holy
things. So *Saul* notwithftanding his Plea
of *neceffity for want of a Prieft,* and the
Danger of falling into the Hands of his
Enemies before he had made *his Peace*
with God, had his Kingdom rent from
him for prefuming *only* to offer a Sacrifice
himfelf, it being none but the Priefts Office

fo to do.   More Examples of this kind
might be brought, but thefe I think are
fufficient to fhew, that God fet fuch a
mighty value upon the *Commiffion* he gave
to *fome Orders of Men*, that he would not
accept of even his own Appointments
when they were *prophan'd* by 𝔲𝔫𝔥𝔞𝔩𝔩𝔬𝔴𝔢𝔡,
𝔲𝔫𝔠𝔬𝔪𝔪𝔦𝔣𝔣𝔦𝔬𝔫𝔢𝔡 Hands :   and what is
this, but to make the *Divine Commiffion* to
be an *Effential* Part of fuch Pofitive Inftitutions ? infomuch, that if any fhould have
knowingly concurr'd with thofe who *ufurp-*
ed it, they would have made themfelves
𝔭𝔞𝔯𝔱𝔞𝔨𝔢𝔯𝔰 in the Sin, as well as th
Punifhment of the Ufurpers ; as we fee
was exemplify'd in the Cafe of *Corah* and
his Company, for no lefs than fourteen
thoufand feven hundred of them were
deftroy'd by a Plague, befides the great
Number of thofe who were before fwallow'd alive into the Earth, and burnt with
Fire from the Lord :   and if fo, may we
not juftly infer that God is ftill as Jealous
of *This Honour* under the Gofpel, the
Minifters whereof being of fo much greater Dignity, by how much the Gofpel is
more excellent than the Law of *Mofes.*
It is certain that even now in the *Chriftian*
Difpenfation, No Man can take this Honour
to himfelf but he that is called of God, as

was Aaron ; and *Aaron's* call was not *by his great Gifts,* and the inward *Dictates* of the *Spirit,* but by an **External Commiſſion** firſt given by God himſelf to *Moſes,* and then by *Moſes,* at the Command of God to *Aaron.* But

Secondly, The Example of our Saviour's not taking upon him to Miniſter in Holy things between God and Man, till he was particularly and *externally Commiſſion'd* by God for that purpoſe; is a further advance towards proving that the Divine Authority of the Adminiſtrator of Baptiſm, is an Eſſential Part of this Inſtitution. For, notwithſtanding he was full of the Holy Ghoſt, which was not given by Meaſure but entirely to him; notwithſtanding his Manhood was inſeperably united to the Second Perſon of the moſt glorious Trinity, whereby he was more than ſufficiently, nay, infinitely *gifted* for ſuch a purpoſe; and notwithſtanding the great Neceſſities, and conſequent Miſeries of all Mankind, which were continually wanting his Undertaking to Adminiſter for them in things pertaining to God; yet he kept himſelf in his *private Station* for about 30 Years together, and never would take upon himſelf ſo *High an Office,*
till

till he receiv'd his Commission and Inauguration thereinto, from the Hands of a Prophet [*John the Baptist*] who Baptiz'd him, to fulfil this Part *of Righteousness* and *Justice, viz.*, of not taking upon himself to be a Minister of the New Covenant, without a special Warrant from *God* by the Mediation of one, who was *by him* appointed to convey this Power and Authority to him : And then we find, that God himself by the Descent of the Holy Ghost upon him in a *visible Glory*, and by *an audible Voice* from Heaven, saying, *This is my Beloved Son in whom I am well pleas'd,* confirm'd his great Commission ; and that from thence forward, *(and not before)* he proceeded in the Execution of it : From that time he preach'd and taught, gave his Apostles order to Baptize and Preach; wrought Miracles himself, and gave others Power to do so likewise, for the Confirmation of his Doctrine, *&c.* Now what should be the Reason of our Saviour's thus long *desisting* from the performance of such beneficial Offices ? Was he not sufficiently *gifted?* Yes certainly he was. Did not the *Extream Miseries* of Man's Spiritual Bondage call loudly for relief ? beyond all doubt they did. Why then did not even *Compassion* it self, the Blessed

Jesus

Jefus, then perfonally among them, undertake their fpeedy Refcue ? Was it becaufe his Hour was not yet come ? Doubtlefs it was not come ; but why ? becaufe he had not yet receiv'd his **Commiffion** from his Father. So that, if our Lord's Example may be allow'd in this Cafe to be Conclufive, it is plain, that not all the *Gifts* imaginable, nor all the *preffing Neceffities* that may be pleaded, can ever of themfelves give fufficient Warrant to Minifter *Authoritativly*, for Men, in things pertaining to God, when thofe things are of fuch a Nature, as that a *Commiffion* from him muft be firft obtain'd by the Perfon who undertakes to Adminifter : And that therfore fuch a Perfon ought to be *duly Commiffion'd* for fuch Adminiftrations. Now that Chriftian Baptifm is fuch an Inftitution as *neceffarily* requires, and *conftantly fuppofes* the Divine Authority of the Adminiftrator, I fhall endeavour to Demonftrate

Thirdly, From the Words of Inftitution ; and in order thereto 'twill be very well worth while to obferve, that our Saviour a little before his Afcenfion into Heaven, appointed the **Eleven Apoftles** and **them only** (notwithftanding the vaft

E Number

Numbers of other Diſciples which he had
at the ſame time,) to go to a particular
Mountain in *Galilee*, which he had told
them of, (St. *Mat* 28. 16.) Where when
they were aſſembl'd he came to them, and
firſt aſſerted *his own Power and Authority*
wherewith he was Inveſted, to Authorize
and Commiſſion them for the *Great Office*
he was then going to confer on them,
ſaying, *All Power is given unto me in Heaven and in Earth,* ver. 18. Whereby he
ſufficiently aſſur'd them, that they might
reſt ſecure and ſatisfy'd, that *The Commiſſion* he was going to give them was of
full Force and Virtue, and ſufficiently Valid to empower them to Act for the future
according to the *Contents* therof ; and
indeed the great things he was about to
Authorize them to do, were of ſo un-
common a Nature, and of ſuch vaſt Con-
ſequence to Mankind, that they might
very well have doubted even of the *ſuf-
ficiency* of their Commiſſion, if our Lord
had not thus fix'd their Faith in *his Power
and Authority* to give it them : when therfore he had thus prepar'd their Minds, he
then proceeds to give them *This Commiſſion*
as the *Conſequent* of that *Power* which
was given him over all things ; ſaying, **Go ye therfore** and Teach (or ra
ther)

ther) **Disciple All Nations, Baptizing them in the Name of the Father, and of the Son, and of the Holy Ghost,** *teaching them to observe all things whatsoever I have commanded you;* **And lo I am with you alway, even unto the end of the World.** These are the Words of Institution of Baptism, wherein 'tis clear at first sight, that the *Eleven Apostles* were the *peculiar Persons* to whom the *Authority* of Baptizing was committed [*Go ye*] and not only they, but also all those who should succeed them, to the end of the World; [*Lo I am with you alway, even unto the end of the World*] for our Saviour's Promise to be with them *so long,* cannot possibly be meant of their *particular Persons* which were not to live to the end of the World, and therfore it must signify the *Apostles* in another Sense, *viz.* those whom **they** and **their Successors** should Appoint throughout all Ages.

SO that by the Words of Institution above recited, it plainly appears, that as long as the World shall last *The Apostles and their Successors* are the Persons *Commission'd* to Disciple the Nations, *Baptizing* them; and hereby 'tis *necessarily imply'd*, that *as often* as this *One Baptism* is perform'd, *so often* 'tis done by *One* who

has

has this *Commiſſion* given to him ; otherwiſe the Promiſe of being with ſuch *Commiſſion'd Perſons* to the end of the World,
would have been *in vain* and of no neceſſity : And if it were not *deſign'd* by
the Inſtitution, that *Baptizing* ſhould be
perform'd to the end of the World by
a Succeſſor of the Apoſtles *or* his *Subſtitute* ;
it might for the *very ſame Reaſon* be ſaid,
that *teaching* was not deſign'd to be by
ſuch a *Succeſſor* to the end of the World,
and ſo the *whole Commiſſion* would be but
Temporary, and conſequently the **Miniſters**
of Chriſt, and **Baptizing** and **Teaching**
would be but *Temporary* ; and Chriſt's Promiſe of being with his Apoſtles in theſe
their Miniſtrations to the end of the World
would have been made without any deſign
of fulfilling it, which is a *Blaſphemous Contradiction* to the Infallible Veracity of our
Bleſſed Lord ; and therfore *as long* as the
World ſhall laſt, ther muſt be *Baptizing,*
and as long as ther ſhall be Baptizing,
ther muſt be *ſuch a One* to perform it, as
Chriſt has promis'd to be with, *viz. a
Succeſſor to the Apoſtles or his Subſtitute,* to
the utmoſt bounds of that Duration.

THIS will further appear from the
Nature of a *Commiſſion,* which is *excluſive* of all others, but thoſe to whom it

                                                       is

is given ; for 'tis well known that when a Prince gives *a Commiffion* to any of his Subjects for the executing of fome *great Office*, it is with defign to *appropriate* that Office to that particular Subject, that *none* may act in it but he, and thofe whom he fhall Authorize : So here *The Commiffion* of Baptizing, *&c.* given by our Saviour to his *Apoftles and their Succeffors* to the end of the World, is *exclufive* of all others, and confequently none can act therin but fuch as they fhall Authorize for that purpofe ; and therfore it neceffarily follows that the *Adminiftrator* of Baptifm muft have the *Divine Commiffion* or Authority, before he prefume to Act in this fo *Appropriate* an Office and Miniftration.

BUT the Form of Adminiftring Baptifm (*in the Name of the Father, and of the Son, and of the Holy Ghoft*) being Effential, for *even the Validity* therof, is an Invincible Argument for the *Divine Authority* of the *Adminiftrator*, that it fhould be alfo an *Effential Part* of this Inftitution, becaufe, as often as any one Adminifters Baptifm *truly* and *really* in the Name of the Trinity, fo often he *exprefly* affirms, and that *truly too*, that he does it by Virtue of that Power and Authority which he receiv'd from the Trinity for fo doing ;

This

This will be evident beyond Contradiction, when we impartially Enquire into the
juſt Meaning and common Acceptation of
the Expreſſion [*In the Name of*] when
us'd by one who Acts for another ; which
we ſhall conſtantly find ſignifies, that he
who comes, and does any thing in another's Name, do's it by his Power and
Authority who ſent him. " Thus *Bleſſed*
" *be he that cometh in the Name of the Lord*,
(*Pſal.* 118. 26.) is the ſame, as Bleſſed be
he whom the Lord hath *Sent*, or who
comes with the *Authority and Commiſſion*
which the Lord hath given him. So
" *When* David's *young Men came, they ſpake*
" *to* Nabal *according to all thoſe words, in*
" *the Name of* David (1 *Sam.* 25. 9.) 'tis
no more than if it had been ſaid, they
ſpake to *Nabal* according to all thoſe
Words, and made uſe of *David's* Name
to let *Nabal* know that he *Sent* them. Thus
again, " Haggai *the Prophet,* &c. *prophe-*
" *ſied unto the Jews, in the Name of the*
" *God of Iſrael*, (*Ezra* 5 1.) What is this
but to ſay that *Haggai* propheſied what
God had *Sent*, and *Order'd* him to Pro-
pheſy to 'em ? When our Saviour ſays,
" *I am come in my Father's Name* (*John*
5. 43.) He plainly declares that he was
Sent by his Father, or came by his parti-
                                          cular

cular Appointment. And Laftly, (To Name no more Texts to this purpofe) when our Bleffed Lord affirms, " *The* " *Works that I do in my Fathers Name* " *they bear Witnefs of me* (*John* 10. 25.) he in plain Terms afferts, that he did thofe Works by Virtue of that *Power* and *Authority* which he had receiv'd from his Father. So when a Magiftrate declares that he Acts *in the Name* of his Prince, every one immediately underftands therby that he Acts by the *Authority* which he receiv'd from him ; but this is too plain to want more Examples ; and therfore we may juftly conclude that every time the Minifter fays, *I Baptize thee in the Name of the Father, and of the Son, and of the Holy Ghoft* ; it is the fame as to fay, I Baptize thee by Virtue of that *Authority* and *Commiffion* which I have receiv'd from the Father, the Son, and the Holy Ghoft ; and therfore when he Baptizes a Perfon, and pronounces the Words, *In the Name of the Father,* &c. if he be one who is *not vefted* with the Divine Authority, he cannot be truly faid to Baptize in the Name of the Trinity, for 'tis a perfect *Contradiction* to fay fuch a thing is truly done in the *Name of another,* when really it is not done *in his Name,* or by his *Au-*

thority

thority and *Commiffion*, which is the only intelligible way of doing fomething in another's Name

THUS we fee how our Lord has infeperably United the *Divine Authority* of the *Adminiftrator*, with the truth and reality of the *Form of Adminiftration*, infomuch, That the Form it felf is no further true, as to the defign therof, than as it is attended with the Truth and Reality of the *Divine Commiffion* given to him who Adminifters ; fo that whenfoever this Form is truly us'd according to the Intent of this Inftitution, the Divine Authority and Commiffion of him who Adminifters, is *neceffarily* and *conftantly* implied and fuppos'd.

AND really if we examine into all the *Divine Pofitive Inftitutions* that ever were made, we fhall find none of them fo indifpenfibly require the *Divine Authority* of the Adminiftrator, and attended with fuch a *Solemn Form* of Afferting and Declaring his Authority *every time* of Adminiftration, as we find in the Divine Pofitive Inftitution of Chriftian Baptifm ; and confequently the Divine Authority of the Adminiftrator of Baptifm is an *Effential Part* of that great Inftitution.

BUT

BUT here I expect some will tell me, that I lay too much stress upon the Form of Administring Baptism, *In the Name* of the Trinity ; because in the *Greek* it is said, *Go ye*, &c. Baptizing them *Into the Name* (instead of *In the Name*) of the Father, &c. and tho' *In the Name* signifies *by the Authority and Commission* of the Trinity, yet *Into the Name* do's not signify So, but rather into the Belief and Service of the Trinity ; which do's not imply so necessarily the Divine Authority of the Administrator as I plead for.

TO whom I Answer, that tho' the *Greek* do's signifie *Into the Name*, yet it do's not therfore follow that this is the *Only* Sense of the Word in the Original Language, wherein St. *Matthew* wrote his Gospel, which the best Criticks affirm was *Hebrew*, or *Syra-Chaldaick*, the Language of the Jews in our Saviour's time, whereof the *Greek* is but a Translation. 'Tis certain that the Universal Church of Christ has in all Ages retained, and constantly practic'd the Form *In the Name* of the Trinity ; and all Antient and Modern Translations from the *Greek* it self, have inserted in the Text of the Institution, *In the Name*, rather than *Into the Name* ; which plainly intimates that the Former

Former · is the most Genuin Sense of St.
Matthew's Original Word, and consequently, sufficiently Authorizes me to lay so
great a stress upon the usual Form of Administring Baptism *in the Name* of the
Trinity, which necessarily supposes the
Administrator therof to be Vested with
the Divine Power and Commission, wherein I am the more confirm'd by the 26th Article of the Church of *England*, which expresly affirms, that the Administrator do'p
·Minister by " *Christ's Commission and Au*
" *thority.*

Dr. *Hammond* indeed in his Practical Catech. *Lib. 6. S.* 2 mentions the *Greek* [*into*
the Name] but then he applies it only to
the Part of the Person Baptized, and says,
that it signifies, " *That he devotes and de*
" *livers himself up to be ruled as an obe*
" *dient Servant, by the Directions of this*
" *great Master, a willing Disciple of this*
" *Blessed Trinity* : But this is nothing to
our present purpose, which is only to enquire, what the Form of Administration
signifies on the Ministers Part ; and this
the same Author tells us in the forecited
place, *viz.* " *That the Words* [*I Baptize*
" *thee in the Name of the Father, and of*
" *the Son, and of the Holy Ghost*] *being*
" *prescrib'd by Christ to his Disciples* (*i. e.*
" *Apostles*)

" *Apoftles*) *muft indifpenfibly, be us'd by all*
" *in the Administration, and the meaning*
" *of them on the Minifters Part, is, that*
" *what he does, he do's not of himfelf, but*
" **in the Name** *or Power of, or by Com-*
" *miffion from the Bleffed Trinity.*

N A Y, tho' the Minifter in Baptizing
fhould fay, I Baptize thee *into the Name*
of the Father, *&c.* (which would be contrary to the Univerfal Form) yet even
then he would therby affert the Divine
Commiffion by which he Acted; becaufe
on his Part, Baptizing the Perfon *into the
Name*, muft fignify that by that Action
he admits him *into the Service* of the Bleffed Trinity; which being a Service of
Infinite Benefit, and attended with In-
eftimable *Supernatural* Rewards to the
Perfon admitted; muft neceffarily fuppofe
the Perfon admitting to be Vefted with a
particular Power and fupernatural Authority for fo great a Purpofe ; Becaufe, *no
Natural Power or Authority*, is fufficient
to confer any the leaft *Supernatural* Benefit or Advantage. But this Truth will be
further confirm'd by the Arguments that
may be drawn,

Fourthly, From the *Defign* and *Benefits*
of Chriftian Baptifm. For by the Words
of

of Inſtitution 'tis plain, that the Deſign therof is to *Diſciple* all Nations, (St. *Mat.* 28.) or which is the ſame thing, to *enter* them into the Church of Chriſt, which in ſeveral Places of Sacred Scripture is called the *Kingdom* of God, and the *Kingdom* of Heaven : Now 'tis evident to whom our Saviour gave the *Keys* of the Kingdom of Heaven, *viz.* to his Apoſtles expreſly, and in *them* to their *Succeſſors*, and conſequently that he gave to them, and thoſe only whom they ſhould Authorize the Supernatural Power of admitting Perſons into the Church by Baptiſm, which is the only Rite of Initiation into this Sacred Society.

ONE of the great Priviledges of True Chriſtian Baptiſm, is, that it is for the *Forgiveneſs of Sins* ; this is a ſupernatural Benefit, and therfore it may be juſtly ask'd, Who can forgive Sins but *God only* ? and if none can, then certainly no Man can aſſume to himſelf the Power of *Conveying* this Forgiveneſs of Sins to others by the *Means* of Baptiſm, except he be endow'd for that purpoſe with Power from *on High*, even from *God* himſelf ; and if any ſhould without the Divine Commiſſion, ſuppoſe himſelf to have this Power, 'tis plain that his Miniſtrations muſt be ineffectual

for

for so great a purpose, because he is destitute of the Divine Character ; he do's not truly personate God the Bestower of this great Priviledge, but runs without being sent ; and God has not any where either by Promise or Covenant oblig'd himself to Ratifie and Confirm the Precipitate Acts, and Usurp'd Administrations of such Rash and Presumptuous Undertakers ; but we know to whom our Lord gave this Authority, *viz.* to his Apostles (and therfore will confirm their Acts) when he said, " *Whosoever Sins ye remit,* " *they are remitted unto them,* and therfore *they only,* and such as they appoint, can *Mediately* remit Sins by Christian Baptism.

ANOTHER *great Priviledge of Christian Baptism is, that those who receive it are therby intitul'd to all the unspeakable Advantages of Free Denizens of Heaven,* notwithstanding that before they were *Aliens* and *Strangers,* and therfore had no Claim, nor any Right or Title to this Freedom. Now let any Man but seriously reflect how unreasonable 'twould be for a Stranger and Foreigner in any State or Kingdom, to imagine that every, even *Natural Subject* there, could have Authority to grant him a *Valid Naturalization,* and

and therby endow him with all the
Rights and *Immunities* which the Free'
Born Subjects of that State or Kingdom
do enjoy ; would it not be Ridiculous
for him to accept (knowingly) of such a
pretended Naturalization ? and if he
should ; can it be thought reasonable, that
he should enjoy all the Advantages annex'd to a True and Lawful Naturalization, to be receiv'd from the Hands of those
only who are Authoriz'd for that purpose ?
certainly No ; never a well Regulated
State or Kingdom in the World, that has
Laws for Naturalizing Strangers, would'
allow it ; and shall it then be once thought,
that *every Subject*, of how mean a Station
soever he be in this Spiritual Kingdom of'
God, can have Authority to Intitle *Strangers* to all the *supernatural* Advantages
which are consequent to a *Legal and Valid*
Naturalization ?

AND indeed all the Benefits and Priviledges of True Christian Baptism are
so great and *many*, that it would be endless to recount them, let it suffice to say,
that it is a Sign, a Seal, a means of Conveyance, and a *Pledge* to assure us of these
Supernatural Advantages, *viz.* of being
Incorporated into the *Houshold*, and therby made *Members* of Christ, *Children* of
God;

God, and *Heirs* of the Kingdom of Heaven, and of all the unspeakable Happynesses therof, which Eye hath not seen, nor Ear heard, neither have enter'd into the Heart of Man to Conceive.

NOW if any reasonable unprejudic'd Man will but duly reflect on these so inconceiveable and inestimable Priviledges, so infinitely above all the Powers of Nature, either to Obtain or Bestow, without some supernatural Donation, 'twill be very difficult, nay, I may say, *impossible* for him to believe, that God, who is the God of Order, and not of *Confusion*, will bestow them by the *Mediation* of those to whom he has given no Authority for that Purpose : Especially when he remembers that God has set apart a *Peculiar Order* of Men to be *the Stewards* of these his *Mysteries*, and to whom he has giv'n the Power of the *Keys*, whereby to admit into, and exclude out of his Spiritual Kingdom, as the Sacred Scripture do's sufficiently inform us: These Men he has dignify'd with *extraordinary Marks* and signal Characters of *Honour*, and *separated* them from the rest of *Mankind* ; that they might *represent his Sacred Presence* among us, and that we might have a *strong Confidence* and well-grounded Assurance of their *Divine Mission*, and

and of our own Happinefs in being admitted through Baptifm into the Number
and Priviledges of his Children, by their
Authoriz'd Miniftration ; for which Reafons, added to thofe others I have brought
under this 4th Head, we may truly fay,
That the Divine Authority of him who
Adminifters Baptifm is an Effential part
of that Holy Inftitution. But this is confirm'd alfo

Fifthly, By the conftant Practice of
thofe who *truly* are, and of others who
pretend to be the Lawful Minifters of the
Chriftian Church.

THE *Lawful Minifters* in all Ages
have claim'd the Authority of Baptizing,
even from the time of our Saviour's firft
giving the Commiffion to his Eleven Apoftles, unto this Day ; and for this *very
Reafon*, becaufe they *Deriv'd* their Minifterial Power and Authority from Chrift ;
but if the Divine Authority of the Adminiftrator of Baptifm were not an Effential Part of that Inftitution, their Claim
would have been unjuft when founded
upon their *Divine Right*, and fo every
Man would have had as much Authority
to Baptize as they : but forafmuch as they
were never accus'd of Injuftice for making

ing this Claim, (except by such Wretches as the Author of the Rights, *&c,* who would confound all Order in the Christian Church;) and since all Sober Christians, who *know* their Duty, never laid Claim to this Authority; it necessarily follows that the Lawful Minister's Claim is good, and consequently that the Divine Authority of him who Administers is an Essential Part of Baptism.

AS for those who *pretend* to be, but are not, the Lawful Ministers of Christ, 'tis well known, that they plead for the Authority of Baptizing upon this very score, that they *esteem* their Ministerial Commission to be of *Divine Right*; and therfore will never suffer their *Common People* to Administer Baptism; from whence it follows, that they also *in practice* confirm this Assertion of the Divine Authority of the Administrator of Baptism: otherwise their claiming the Power of Baptizing, by Virtue of the *suppos'd Divine Right* of their Mission, would be a meer foolery, and indeed a Contradiction.

SO that the Lawful Minister's claiming the Authority of Baptizing, because his Mission is *truly* of Divine Right; and the unlawful Minister's Claiming the same Authority because he *esteems* his Mission

F   also

also to be of Divine Right, do both con-
spire by their Practice to Confirm this
Truth, that the Divine Authority of the
Administrator of Baptism is an Essential
Part of that Holy Institution; and this is
not a little Corroborated,

Sixthly and Lastly, From the Doctrine
and Practice of the Church of *England*.

For in her 23d. Article of Religion, she
affirms, That " *it is not Lawful* for *any*
" *Man* to take upon him the Office *of Mi-*
" *nistring the Sacraments*, &c. before he
" be *Lawfully call'd and Sent* to execute
" the fame. Now what can this Article
mean by [*it is not Lawful ?*] Certainly
nothing else but that *it is Sinful*, or Contrary to the Divine Law in the Holy Scripture, for she is not treating of *Civil*, but
Spiritual things. But against what Law
in the Sacred Scriptures is this a Sin? furely against *that Law* which treats of *these*
Sacraments, and this Law is principally
in the Institution of them; so that the
plain meaning of this Article must be,
that it is *contrary* to the very Institution
of the *Sacraments* for *any Man* to take
upon him " the Office of Administring
" them, before he be *Lawfully call'd and*
" *sent to execute the same.*

AND

AND in her 26th Article, she teaches " that the Administrators of the Sa-" craments do not Minister in their own " Name but in Christ's, and by his *Com-" mission and Authority*

AND least every One who has acquir'd (tho' not justly) the Reputation of being such a Lawful Minister, should fancy himself to have *Christ's Commission,* because the People made choice of him, and some others of higher Rank among them, took upon them to Ordain him, Separate from, and Independent of the Bishop ;

In the Preface to her Form and Manner of Making, Ordaining, and Consecrating of Bishops, Priests, and Deacons, she tells us thus, " It is evident unto all Men " *diligently* reading *Holy Scripture,* and " Antient Authors, that *from the Apostles* " *time* there have been these Orders of " Ministers in Christ's Church, *Bishops,* " *Priests* and *Deacons*; which Offices were " evermore had in such Reverend Esti-" mation, that *no Man* might presume to " execute *any* of them, except he ——— " by Publick Prayer, with Imposition of " Hands, were approv'd, and admitted " thereunto by *Lawful Authority.* [And whic she means by this *Lawful Authority*

F 2   is

is plain by the words immediately follow-
ing] " And therefore, *&c.* *No Man* shall
" be accounted, or taken to be a Lawful
" Bishop, Priest, or Deacon, in the Church
" of *England*, or suffer'd to execute any
" of the said Functions, except he be
" call'd, *&c.* thereunto, according to the
" Form hereafter following, **or hath had**
" **formerly Episcopal Consecration, or**
" **Ordination** ; whereby she confines the
lawful Authority, so evidently to Episcopacy ; that a Man must be wilfully blind
who dares to deny it.

  ALL which put together, sufficiently
prove that by the Doctrine of this Church,
the Divine Authority of the Administrator of Christian Sacraments, is an Essential Part of their Institution ; and consequently, that the Divine Authority of the
Administrator of Baptism (which is one
of those Sacraments) must be also an Essential Part of that Holy Institution.

  SO likewise by her Practice she confirms this Truth ; for in her Office of Or-
dering of Priests, the Bishop says to the
Priest : " Receive the Holy Ghost for
" the Office and Work of *a Priest* in the
" Church of God *now committed unto thee*
" by the Imposition of our Hands. Whose
" Sins thou dost Forgive, they are For-
                                    " given;

" given; and whose Sins thou dost retai ,
" they are retained. And be thou a
" faithful Dispenser of the Word of God,
" and *of his Holy Sacraments*, in the Name
" of the Father, and of the Son, and of
" the Holy Ghost, *Amen*. And delivering
to the Priest kneeling, the Bible into his
Hand, the Bishop adds, " *Take thou* **Au**
' **thority** *to Preach the Word of God, and*
" *to Minister the Holy Sacraments.* By all
which 'tis plain, that she reckons the Administration of the Sacraments to be *Ef-*
sential to the Office of the Priest, and
that he must have **Co** *mission* even from
the Holy Trinity, by the Mediation of
the Bishop, convey'd to him, to Qualifie
and Authorize him to Administer the
same. And in Conformity to this her
Rule of Practice, when any Person, tho'
formerly a *Teacher*, and one who has
assum'd to himself before, the Power of
Baptizing and Administring the *Lord's*
Supper, notwithstanding his having continu'd even in the *Tolerated* Practice of
these Usurpations for many Years together, nay, tho' chosen therto by the Consent of *the People* who submitted to and
acknowledg'd all such his Ministrations to
be *Valid and Good*, when such a Man I say
forsakes his *Heresies*, or *Schisms*, and re-

turns, or defires to be United to her Communion, and to be reckon'd in the number, and to have Licenfe to act as one, of *her Lawful Minifters*, fhe will not allow him fuch a *Licenfe*, he muft be receiv'd only to *Lay Communion*, if he was never before *Divinely Authoriz'd* by *Impofition of Epifcopal Hands*, and now refufes to accept fuch *Catholick Ordination* : She therby declares that he wants the *Divine Commiffion* to act in fuch Holy Miniftrations, and that fhe will not acquiefce with his former Ufurpations, he muft *difclaim* and *renounce* them now, if in her Communion he would be allow'd to Officiate in the Word and Sacraments, as the reft of her Minifters do. But why all this, if his Power and Authority had been *fufficient* before, for the Purpofes of the Holy Sacraments ? if his Commiffion was good then, 'tis fo now, and 'tis needlefs to *Re-ordain* him ; but if it was *Invalid*, fhe acts confiftent with her felf in refufing to admit him among her Minifters, **to whom alone** fhe gives Authority for thefe great purpofes. And really it ought not to be diffembl'd, that if fuch a Man's Adminiftrations of the Sacraments were before *agreeable* to, and not *breaches* of their Inftitution, His Miniftry before was

                                    alfo

alſo *Valid,* and therfore 'twould be even *unjuſt* to require him to take up a *new Commiſſion,* and from **another ſort** of Authority than what he had receiv'd it from at firſt ; becauſe, the Deſign of handing down Chriſt's Commiſſion to Miniſters, in all *Ages,* is, that ther may be conſtantly *ſuch Perſons* to Adminiſter the Holy Sacraments, as he in the firſt Inſtitution of thoſe Sacraments did Authorize and Require : but foraſmuch as the Church of *England* requires ſuch Perſons, as above mention'd, to receive the *Divine Authority,* which ſhe reckons they wanted before, to qualify them for the Adminiſtration of Sacraments, 'tis plain that this her Practice diſcourages us to hope, that without the Divine Authority they are qualify'd for ſuch Miniſtrations ; and conſequently confirms us in this, that the *Divine Commiſſion* of the Adminiſtrator is an Eſſential Part of the Inſtitution of a Sacrament. Nay, ſo very Cautious is ſhe, not to allow the *contrary,* that ſhe makes not ſo much as any exception for Caſes of *Abſolute Neceſſity,* no not tho' an Unbaptiz'd Perſon were giving up the Ghoſt, ſhe has not declar'd that any one may Baptize him but the *Miniſter of the Pariſh,* or in his Abſence any other *Lawful Miniſter* that.

F 4   can

can be procur'd ; as in her Office for *private Baptism*, which is the only Office she has provided for Cafes of Neceffity : and what she means in the Rubrick therof, by *Lawful Minister*, is eafily determin'd by her 26th Article of Religion, *viz* " *One who Ministers in Christ's Name,* " *and by his Commiffion and Authority.*

AND now to fum up all that has been faid under thefe Six Heads.

FORASMUCH as God under the *Mofaic Difpenfation* which was but the *fore-runner* of the *Chriftian*, made the *Divine Authority* of the Adminiftrator an Effential Part of his then Pofitive Inftitutions, infomuch as not to accept of the performance of the *latter* without the *former* : Forafmuch as Chrift himfelf, notwithftanding his own *Perfonal Excellencies* and *Perfections*, and the preffing *Neceffities* of the whole World, which ftood in need of his Miniftrations, would not leave his *private Station* to take upon him fo great an Office till duly Authoriz'd by the *Divine External Commiffion* : Forafmuch as in the Words of the Inftitution of Baptifm, our Lord Commiffion'd *no other* than his Eleven Apoftles and their Succeffors

fors and Subſtitutes to Baptize to the End
of the World : Foraſmuch as their Commiſſion (as all others are) is *Excluſive* of
all, but thoſe to whom 'twas given; and
the very Form of Adminiſtration of Baptiſm, *in the Name,* or by *the Authority* of
the Trinity requires and neceſſarily ſup-
poſes and implies the *Divine Authority* of
him who Adminiſters : Foraſmuch as the
Berefits of Baptiſm are ſo great and **Su**
pernatural, that none can give or *convey*
them by Baptiſm, but ſuch as God has
appointed : Foraſmuch as all who call
themſelves the Divinely Authoriz'd Miniſters of the Chriſtian Church, have in
all Ages claim'd the Power of Baptizing
upon the Account of their *Divine Com-*
miſſion : and laſtly, Foraſmuch as the
Church of *England* by her *Doctrine* and
Practice, gives ſufficient ground to believe
that none can Adminiſter Sacraments but
thoſe who are *Divinely Authoriz'd* for
that purpoſe, and that to pretend to do
ſo, is contrary even to the very Inſtitution
of the Chriſtian Sacraments : ſeeing all
theſe premiſes are true, and not to be deny'd, without running into unavoidable
Inconſiſtencies and Contradictions, it muſt
neceſſarily be granted, that the *Divine*
Authority of the Adminiſtrator of Baptiſm

IS

is an *Essential Part* of that Holy Institution, to be observ'd as *often* and *as long* as Baptism shall be necessary to be Administer'd, *even* to the End of the World.

PROPOSITION II.

THAT every Essential Part of Christian Baptism ; (*viz* The *Divine Authority* of the Administrator, *The Water, and the Form of Administration* in the Name of the Trinity) is of equal Obligation and Necessity to us.

DEMON. This will follow from the first Proposition of the Introduction ; which I shall apply to this Divine Positive Institution : for the very Nature of this Institution is such, that it had no *Intrinsick Excellency,* or Moral Virtue, either in the *Person Baptizing,* or in *the Water,* or in the *Form of Words* wherewith Baptism is given, to bind or oblige us to observe the same, till the Divine Command laid that Necessity upon us, as indeed we find it did ; so that now we are oblig'd to observe this Institution purely *and only* by Virtue of this *Divine Command,* which, forasmuch as it extends it self to *every one* of the said *Essential Parts* therof (as has

been

been prov'd in the preceeding Propofition, wherein 'twas Demonftrated, *That the Divine Authority of the Adminiftrator of Baptifm is an Effential Part thereof as well as the Water and the Form)* will make them all of *equal Authority,* and confequently of *equal Neceffity* and *Obligation* to us; becaufe, the *Divine Authority* of the Adminiftrator, the *Water,* and the *Form* of Adminiftration are every one of them diftinctly of the fame Nature (*i. e.* but meer Pofitive Inftitutes) as the whole Inftitution it felf. And again, being all Effential Parts [*or fuch as are conftantly to be obferv'd as long as the Ordinance of Baptifm fhall be obliging*] 'tis evident that for the fame Reafon as one part may be omitted, another may be fo likewife, and confequently that every one of them is upon *all Accounts whatfoever,* of equal Obligation and Neceffity to us. *Q. E. D.*

COROLLARY.

HENCE it follows, that as no Humane Authority can *Difpenfe* with the whole Inftitution of Baptifm, where 'tis binding and obliging (*Axiom* 3.) fo neither can they Difpenfe with the Omiffion of either Water. or the Form of Adminiftration,

niſtration, in the Name of the Trinity, or the *Divine Miſſion* of him who Adminiſters : Nor can any ſuch Authority de-
termine that one of theſe Eſſential Parts
of the Adminiſtration of Baptiſm, is
more excellent than another, becauſe they
have every one diſtinctly, the ſame Authority Commanding, from which *alone* they
receive their whole Force and Efficacy,
and are *only* by Virtue of *that one Authority*, made equally neceſſary and binding
to us.

PROPOSITION III.

WHOSOEVER affirms Baptiſm to
be *wholly Null* and *Invalid*, by reaſon of
the *Omiſſion* either of *Water*, or of the
Form of Adminiſtring in the Name of the
Trinity, ought alſo for the *ſame Reaſon*
to acknowledge that Baptiſm *is ;as much
Null and Invalid* when it wants *only* the
Divine Authority or Commiſſion of the Adminiſtrator.

DEMON. This will follow from
the ſecond Propoſition of the Introduction.

FOR the *only Reaſon* why the *Omiſſion*
of

of either Water, or the Form, makes such a Baptism Void, must be, because such Omission is *Unlawful*, or *Contrary* to the Institution of Baptism (*Axiom* 4.) So that he must affirm such Baptism Null, because 'tis Administer'd either with such Matter, or Form, as the Institution has not appointed; or, because 'tis not Administer'd with such Matter or Form as the Institution requires; Now forasmuch as Christ, who appointed the Water and the Form, appointed also the Person who should Administer both the one and the other; and since the Divine Authority of this Administrator is an Essential Part, and as much obliging and necessary as Water and the Form, those two other Essential Parts of the Institution, (*by the* 1*st and* 2*d Propositions:*) it must necessarily follow that the want of Divine Authority in him who Administers, is *equally* a Breach of, or *contrary* to, the said Institution; and therfore if the *want* of Water, or the Form, makes any Baptism to be *wholly Null and Void*, because contrary to the Institution; the want also of *only* the Divine Commission in the Administrator, must for the *same Reason* make that Baptism so Minister'd to be *wholly Invalid, and of no Effect*, being *equally* contrary to the

the fame Inftitution : and confequently whofoever affirms Baptifm to be *wholly Null and Invalid*, by reafon of the *Omiffion* either of Water or the Form, ought alfo for the *fame Reafon* to acknowledge that Baptifm *is as much Null and Invalid* when it wants *only* the Divine Authority or Commiffion of the Adminiftrator. *Q. E. D.*

COROLLARY.

FROM this Propofition it undoubtedly follows, that the Invalidity of fuch Baptifms as are Adminifter'd by unauthoriz'd Perfons, cannot be *partial*, but *entire* ; for if Baptifm be wholly void for want of *Water*, or the *Form* of Adminiftring in the Name of the Trinity, as the whole Church of Chrift have conftantly and with great Reafon affirm'd ; it muft be alfo (by this laft Propofition) as *entirely* (and confequently *not partially*) Invalid, for want of *only* the Divine Miffion of the Adminiftrator ; and all this by reafon of the *equal Authority and Neceffity* of every one of thefe Effential Parts.

I mention this, [that ther cannot be any *partial Invalidity*, but it muft be *whole* and *entire*] becaufe I have heard
from

from fome, that the want of the Divine
Miffion of the Adminiftrator of Baptifm,
makes fuch a Baptifm *but partially Invalid* ;
and that, provided the Perfon is Baptized
by fuch a one, with Water, and pronouncing of [*In the Name of the Father, and
of the Son, and of the Holy Ghoft,*] Impofition of the Bifhop's Hand is fufficient
to fupply the other defect ; and confequently to make fuch Baptifm as Valid, as
it would have been, if Adminifter'd by
one *Divinely Authoriz'd,* that is, *wholly
and entirely Valid* : but that this cannot
be, is evident by the above-mention'd
Corollary, wherein 'tis plainly Demonftrated that if in this Cafe ther be any
Invalidity at all, it cannot be *partial* but
entire : and as for the virtue of fuch Impofition of Hands, 'tis utterly contrary
to *Axiom* the 5th, which is a firft
principle, viz. *That no Power or Authority on Earth can by any after Act
(not appointed by God for that purpofe)
make that which before was Invalid, to become as Valid, as Conforming to the Divine
Inftitution it felf would have made it :* So
that, if by *Impofition of Hands,* they
would make fuch Imperfect or Invalid
Baptifms, to be as Valid as the perfect
ones perform'd according to the Inftitution ;

on ; it lies upon them to Demonſtrate;
that ſuch Impoſition of Hands was appointed by *God himſelf*, either in ſome
Law, or by the Practice of the Holy Apoſtles, for ſuch a purpoſe ; but this I De-
ſpair of ever ſeeing them do, becauſe the
Sacred Oracles give us not the leaſt En.
couragement, either in plain Words, or
by good Inferences (to be drawn from
ſuch as are not ſo plain) to believe that
this *Rite* of the Impoſition of Hands;
with reſpect to Baptiz'd Perſons, was ever
Ordain'd, but to be perform'd on thoſe
only; who were before *truly* and *Validily*
Baptiz'd : Ther is not one Example of
the Apoſtles uſing this Ceremony to make
up *ſuch defects* of Baptiſm, nor any thing
like it ; and if in after Ages *ſome* us'd
this Ordinance for that purpoſe (as I find
they did) they ſeem therby to have diſpens'd with a Divine Poſitive Inſtitution
at the ſame time that it was *binding and*
obliging ; which was taking to themſelves
an Authority that did not at all belong to
them (by *Axiom* 3.) I ſay they diſpens'd
with a Divine Poſitive Inſtitution when
'twas binding and obliging, becauſe, they
allow'd of the *Omiſſion* of the *Divine Au-*
thority of the Adminiſtrator of Baptiſm.
which might have been had (and was

ther for

therfore binding and obliging) at the *same time* as they gave Imposition of Hands to such imperfectly Baptized Persons, who might *instead therof*, have been *then* Baptiz'd by themselves or their Substitutes, who were vested with the Divine Authority for that purpose.

AS for the Church of *England* she gives us not the least Intimation of any Efficacy in the Imposition of the Bishop's Hand, to give Validity to such Baptisms, as are suppos'd to be *partly* Invalid before ; for, her Office of Confirmation is made *only* for Persons *Validly Baptized* ; and if they are not so, the use of that Office upon their Account, will be a perfect Contradiction ; because, the Prayer of the Bishop before he blesses by Imposition of his Hand, asserts, ' *That God has* " *Regenerated the Person by Water and the* " *Holy Ghost ; and has given unto him* " *forgiveness of all his Sins,* which takes in the whole Benefit of Valid Baptism, and therfore cannot be said, with any Sense, over a Person whose Baptism is suppos'd to be but *partly Valid,* and consequently to convey but part of the Benefits of True Baptism : So little has she provided for any Method of giving Validity

G to

to partly Invalid Baptisms, as some before her have done.

THE Cause why they would not in those Days give such Persons *Catholick Baptism*, at the Hands of those who were duly Authoriz'd by the *Divine Commission*, was, that they reckon'd *any Baptism* with Water, in the Name of the Trinity, by *whomsoever* Administer'd, to be that *One Baptism* which ought not to be repeated; and yet, at the *same time* they esteemed such a Baptism in some Measure *Invalid*, till it was perfected or rather mended by Imposition of the Bishops Hands; (See the Council of *Eliberis, Anno* 305. Can 33. *Prelim Disc.* pag 12. now who (that seriously considers these things) does not see a great deal of inconsistency in this Matter? for if ther be *But one Baptism* it must certainly be that which has *no Invalidity*, being Administer'd exactly accor'ing to the *Institution*; and therfore those *other Baptisms* which are not so Administer'd, and are therfore confessedly *imperfect* and *partly Invalid*, must be of *another kind* distinct from that *One True Baptism*, and this will introduce *two Sorts* of Baptisms in the Christian Church, which is utterly contrary to their own Assertion, as well as that of the Holy
Scripture

Scripture, which acknowledges no more
than *One Baptism for the Remission of Sins*;
and consequently these imperfect Baptisms
are no Baptisms at all, and so are entirely
void, and of no effect 'And indeed; to
allow the Contrary, is in effect to destroy
the *whole Ministry* of the *Christian Priesthood*; and to open a Door of *Licenti-
ousness* to all Intrudors into that Sacred
Office, and therby put every Man upon a Le-
vel insomuch that at last all may set up for
themselves, and refuse to give any regard or
attention, any deference or respect to our
blessed Lord and Master, in the Person of
his Authoriz'd Ambassadors and Ministers
for where will the Confusion end, if every Man may be suppos'd capable of giving *Valid Baptism?* Will they not argue,
What need we attend upon others for
these Ministrations, when we have as much
Valid Power therin as themselves? if our
Baptisms are Valid, so may our Administrations of the Lord's Supper, and much
more our Preaching to, and Teaching
such People, as we can gather to our
selves: if Validity may be allow'd *to all
these*, by whomsoever Administer'd, then
Farewel all Rule and Order in the Church;
and Christ's setting some therin, first
Apostles; secondaiily *Prophets.* &c. for
G 2   the

the perfecting of the Saints, for the Work
of the Ministry; and his promising to be
with them to the end of the World, was
to no purpose. And it will not serve to
say, that such Men will be guilty of Sin
in those Usurpations, except we say also,
that *their Authoritative Acts of Ministring*
in what they call the Holy Sacraments
are Sins too, and consequently, contrary
to the Institution of the Real Sacraments,
and therfore of *no effect* to convey the
Supernatural Graces and Benefits annex'd
to them: for, if ever Men can be once
perswaded, that *any unauthoriz'd Person*
can by means of the mere *Opus Operatum,*
of what they call Sacraments, convey those
unspeakable Advantages which are annex'd
to Real Sacraments, it will be in vain
for you true **Ministers** to tell them of
the sin of Usurping the Sacred Office,
when *you* in effect assure them, that every
Christian can *Validly* Exercise it; and as
fruitless will it be, to preach to them the
Danger of *Schism* or causeless Separation
from the Church, when you, by allowing the *Validity* of their *Uncommissioned*
Teachers Ministrations or suppos'd Sacraments, give them an Argument to confound all that you shall say for their Conviction, by your affirming that their Sacraments

craments are *as true*, and *effectual* as your own ; and that, (fince they therby receive as much Spiritual Benefit as others do by yours, *becaufe God as much concurs with fuch their Sacraments as with yours*) your charging them with *Schifm* in adhering to *Minifters* who have no *Divine Miffion*, is ridiculous and nonfenfical; becaufe, they have all *as Valid a Commiffion* as your own, which you your felves muft needs grant, by allowing the *Validity* of their fuppos'd Sacraments. Nay further, if it be allow'd that fuch *their Sacraments* are Valid, then *any Excommunicated Perfon* (tho' never Authoriz'd by a Divine Commiffion) if he can but gather a Congregation to himfelf, may fet up for a *Valid Minifter*, and even they who *know this*, may receive *Valid Sacraments* at his Hands, *if the want of a Divine Miffion in the Adminiftrator do's not Invalidate the Sacraments :* Which is a Confequence *fo horrid*, and attended with fuch *infinite Confufions*, that it fhould make fober Chriftians even tremble to think of it · And this brings me to my laft Propofition, *viz.*

PROPOSITION IV.

THAT he who knows himself to have been *Invalidly* Baptiz'd, by one who never had the **Divine Commission**, can have *no just Grounds* to expect the Supernatural *Graces* and Benefits annex'd to the *One True Christian Baptism* ; till he has done *his utmost* for the obtaining of them, by endeavouring to procure *That One Baptism* from the Hands of a *Divinely Authoriz'd Minister.*

DEMON. For, however God may dispense with the **want** of this Sacrament, (*Axiom* 2.) to those who know nothing of it ; such as Infants ; or others who think they have receiv'd it tho' they have not, and would receive it if they could be perswaded that they had not ; or lastly, those who know that they never receiv'd it, and are heartily desirous of it, but cannot possibly attain it: yet, as *he who knows to do good, and do's it not, to him it is Sin* (*Axiom* 6) So he who **knows** that he ought to be Baptiz'd by a Minister vested with the **Divine Authority** for that purpose, and **neglects** to be so Baptiz'd, incurs the guilt of Sin, and consequently,

while

while he *continues* in that guilt, can (by *Axiom* 6.) expect none of the *Supernatural* Benefits annex'd to the due performance of his *neglected Duty* of receiving such *Valid Baptism.* This is so clear and evident that ther is no need to enlarge upon it : Only I would further add, that if he knows himself to be Invalidly Baptiz'd by one who never had the Divine Commission, and who notwithstanding presum'd to Baptize him *in Opposition to* and *Rebellion* against, those who were truly Authoriz'd for that purpose, his acquiescing with such a Baptism will be an Addition to his Sin because he therby makes himself a **partner** in the other's **Rebellion** and strengthens him and his Adherents in their Wickedness of *opposing* Christ's Lawful Ministers, concerning whom our Blessed Lord has positively affirm'd, that, *he who despises them, despises him, and he that despises him, despises him that sent him ;* and what greater Contempt can be offer'd to them, than to take part with such as *oppose* them in all the Ministrations of that Sacred Office to which our Saviour has appointed them ? This should make us exceeding careful not to *concur* with such Men in their *Usurpations,* especially considering that by this our

Con-

Concurrence we involve our selves in the guilt of *Rebellion*, even against God himself; the consequence of which must needs fall *infinitly* short of any the least Advantage, and on the contrary bring upon us the severest of his Wrath, instead of *those Supernatural Graces* and Benefits which he has promis'd to those who duly obey his Holy Institutes.

A S for those who do not, but yet *may know*, whether the Baptism they have receiv'd be according to Christ's Institution, or no, and consequently *Valid* or *not Valid*; it highly concerns them to make use of those Faculties wherewith God has Blessed them, that they may not be deceiv'd in *so great an Affair* as this is.; for, *wilful Ignorance*, and *carelessness* in Spiritual things, will never excuse them at the Day of Judgment, nor will it then serve their turns to plead, that they follow'd the Instructions and Examples of their Teachers; for our Lord, who is Truth it self, has faithfully assur'd us, that *if the Blind lead the Blind, both shall fall into the Ditch*; and the *unprofitable* Servant who improv'd not his Lord's Talent, but hid it in a Napkin, was for his *Sloth* and *Idleness* branded with the dreadful Name of *Wicked,* and cast into outer Darkness,

to

to teach us *Diligence* in the moſt import-
ant things of another Life ; and what
can be of greater Importance to us, than
to know whether we' are trúly *Initiated*
into the Chriſtian Church, and therby intitul'd to all *Thoſe infinite Benefits and
Priviledges*, thoſe ineſtimable Graces and
Bleſſings which every Member of the
Church has a *Right* and *Title* to ? certainly, it highly concerns us to know the
Truth of *our Claim* to ſuch vaſt Benefits,
ſince our Saviour has told us, That *except
a Man be born of Water*, &c. he cannot
enter into the Kingdom of God, he cannot be a Member of that Kingdom here
in the *Church Militant*, the only known
Ark of Salvation from the Wrath to come,
nor in Heaven hereafter, *in the Church
Triumphant*, if thro' his careleſſneſs and
negligence he has not been Really *initiated or enter'd* therinto by that *One Baptiſm*,
which Chriſt has Inſtituted *and Commiſſion'd his Apoſtles and them only, with their
Sucreſſors and their Subſtitutes, to Adminiſter* for that purpoſe, *to the End of the
World.*

AND now having gone thro' all that
I deſign'd to ſay about *Invalid Baptiſm*,
I ſhall conclude with my Anſwers to ſome
few Objections that may probably be
ſtarted againſt this Eſſay. OB-

OBJECTIONS.

Obj. I. SOME may Object, That, tho'
Christ bid his *Eleven Apostles*
Difciple the Nations, *Baptizing them*, &c
yet he did not therfore confine Baptifm to
their, and their Succeffors Miniftration fo, as
that *none* can Adminifter *true Baptifm* but
they, and fuch *only* as they fhall Authorize;
for if he had, he would in exprefs Words
have told us, that no others fhould have
Authority to Baptize but they.

Anfwer, 'Tis Univerfally granted that
our Lord confin'd the *Matter* of Baptifm
to *Water*, and *the Form* to, *In the Name
of the Trinity* ; merely by his faying thefe
Words, *Baptizing them in the Name of the
Father, and of the Son, and of the Holy
Ghoft* : So that no other *Matter* or *Form*
can be introduc'd for the Adminiftration
of *Valid* Baptifm, tho' Chrift has not in
exprefs Words forbidden us to Introduce
them. Even fo, tho' he has no where
faid in exprefs Words, *That none but his
Apoftles, and their Succeffors, and fuch
as they fhould appoint might have this Authority*, yet I affirm, that he has confin'd
true Chriftian Baptifm *to their Miniftration only* ; becaufe, he has done as much

as

as if he had said so in express and positive Words; for he gave *that Commission* **particularly** *to them, and to no others,* and promis'd *constantly to concur with, and support them* in the Exercise therof, *to the End of the World*; and he has made no such romise to Lay Baptizers; and this is as full and express, as his Appointing no other *Matter* than [*Water,*] and no other *Form* than [*In the Name of the Trinity,*] as is very evident to all, who give themselves leave to think justly, and adequately on the Words of *Institution.* Besides, this Commission is of such great Moment, that the Apostles themselves could never have *lawfully* undertaken to Minister in it, if Christ himself had not *particularly Authoriz'd them so to do,* because Baptism is, by virtue *only* of Christ's Institution made a Means of conveying **Supernatural Benefits**, which they had no **natural Right** to confer on any Man by *means therof,* and they could acquire no **Supernatural One** to do so, till Christ gave them that *Power* by a *Particular Designation,* as we find he did, in the very Words of Institution; and therfore, since the Apostles themselves could never have presum'd to act in this great Ministration, without a *Particular Divine Commission*;

it

it being impoſſible for even them to Adminiſter Baptiſm Valid, *for Supernatural
Ends and Purposes*, without it ; it muſt
needs follow, that no others can do ſo,
*but by Virtue of this, or some other new
Commiſſion*, and if they have no *new one,*
they muſt do it by Virtue of *the Old*, and
conſequently, he who Adminiſters Baptiſm, Valid for *Supernatural purpoſes* (**and
'tis not Chriſtian Baptiſm if it be not
thus Valid**, muſt neceſſarily be veſted
with the *Divine Commiſſion*, given at firſt
to the Eleven Apoſtles, and by their Succeſſors convey'd down to him : And if ſo,
then all others are excluded from any *Valid* Miniſtration hereof, becauſe they are
Deſtitute of this Divine Commiſſion, which
was never once given to them for ſuch a
purpoſe.

Obj. II. Others may probably Object,
That at this Rate I confine *the Efficacy* of
the Sacraments, and particularly of Baptiſm, *wholly* to the Divine Authority of
the Adminiſtrator ; and ſo, if the Perſon
who Miniſters, has not been *Commiſſion'd*
by Chriſt, he Adminiſters no *real Sacraments* at all.

Anſ. When the outward Elements of
the Chriſtian Sacraments are *rightly* Adminiſter'd

minister'd according to *all the Essential Parts of their Institution,* then, *and then only,* they become *efficacious* to the Worthy Receiver of them; and this their Efficacy proceeds *only* from God's concurrence with his Promise, made to such due Administration of them: So that in Christian Baptism, the Efficacy depends *no more* upon the Divine *Commission* of him who Administers, than upon the *Water,* and the *Form* of Administration; but upon God's performing his Promise, to bestow the *Supernatural Graces* therof, by the *Mediation of his own Minister's applying the Water in the Name of the Trinity:* And therfore, as the Church has constantly affirm'd, that God do's not give Efficacy to *Water* Administer'd *even by his own Minister,* without the use of these Words [*In the Name of the Father, and of the Son, and of the Holy Ghost*] because an *Essential Part* of the Institution is omitted; So, we have *no Reason* from Divine Revelation (which is our **only Guide** in this Case) to believe, that he will give Efficacy to *Water* Administer'd with the pronouncing of the said *Form* of Words, when 'tis done by *one who has not the Divine Commission* for so doing, because, *this* is also an Omission of *another equally Essential*

sential Part of the same Institution, as I humbly hope I have sufficiently prov'd.

AS to the latter part of this Objection, *viz.* That if the Person who Ministers has not been Commission'd by Christ, he Administers *no real Sacraments* at all; I readily acknowledge that my Discourse do's imply so much; and that the contrary ought *upon no account whatsoever* to be affirm'd or believ'd; because, the outward Elements are not *Sacraments* by themselves, nor made any ways Efficacious for *Supernatural purposes*, till Administer'd as God has appointed in their Institution; and when they are *so Administer'd*, then they become *Sacraments*, and are therby made *Means* of *conveying*, and also *Pledges* to assure us of the *Supernatural Graces* which God has annex'd to such their Administration: Now who do's not see at first sight, that *none* can make any thing to be the *Means* of conveying *supernatural Benefits and Advantages*, who have not the Power and Authority of a *supernatural Commission*? That no Person can make that, which before had no such Excellent Quality, to become *a Pledge* or *An Earnest* of Assurance, that God will grant us such Inestimable Graces, and Priviledges (as Nature could never have Intitul'd us to) except

except he be firſt *ſent, and therby Autho-*
riz'd for that purpoſe, by him who *is to*
acknowledge the *Pledge* as his own, and
for the ſake therof, is to perform all that
was promis'd and imply'd by the giving
and receiving of it ?

As for Inſtance,

IN Chriſtian Baptiſm, *Water,* the outward Element, is no Chriſtian Sacrament
till apply'd as the Inſtitution of Baptiſm
requires, and then, *and then only 'tis a*
Means of *conveying,* and a *Pledge to aſſure*
us of the *Myſtical Waſhing away of Sin* ;
and how ſhall we reſt ſatisfy'd and aſſur'd,
that it is ſuch *a Means and Pledge,* if it
is not apply'd and given to us by 𝕲𝖔𝖉
𝖍𝖎𝖒𝖘𝖊𝖑𝖋 *in the Perſon of his Repreſentative,*
Commiſſion'd by him to give us this Aſſu-
rance ? 'tis certain, that if *Water* be apply'd never ſo ſeriouſly, it cannot be the
Chriſtian Sacrament of Baptiſm, if it wants
the true Form, [*In the Name of the Tri-*
nity,] appointed in the Inſtitution ; this
every one will acknowledge ; and why
then ſhould any plead for its being a Sacrament, when the very Truth of the
Form it ſelf is deſtroy'd, by the Adminiſtration of an Un-Commiſſion'd Perſon,
who

who cannot *really and truly, and without
a Lye* say, 'I Baptize thee in the Name [*or
by the Authority and Commission*] of the
Father, and of the Son, and of the Holy
Ghost ; this his Usurpation *is as contrary*
to the Institution, as a truly Commission'd
Person's leaving out the *Form* wou'd be ;
as I think I have prov'd ; and therfore,
if the one hinders the *Water* from being
a True Christian Sacrament, the other
must do so too, because the *Person* to Administer is *as much appointed*, as *the Matter*
and *Form* of Administration : And this
Person is **as much** the *Representative* of
God the giver, as the *matter* is the *Repre-
sentation* of the Graces given ; insomuch,
that we have at least as much reason to
omit the *Symbolical Element*, as we have
to leave out the Divine Authority *or Commission*, which represents no less than God
himself ; and therfore those Administrations of the *former*, which are destitute of
the *latter*, are no Christian Sacraments or
(which is the same) *Means and Pledges*
of *Supernatural Graces*.

Obj. III. But if this be so (others will
say) you have brought us to a fine pass ;
for 'tis well known that this Divine Authority is very much Controverted, and
where

where to fix it, is not yet determin'd; fo that while we are in this fufpenfe, we muft be always doubting concerning the Validity of our Baptifm, and therby you put this Divine Inftitution upon a very *precarious* and *uncertain* Foundation.

Anf. That the Divine Right of who fhall Minifter in things pertaining to God, has been, and ftill is, very much Difputed by fome *Ignorant* and *Foolifh* Men, and alfo by others of *corrupt Principles* and *wicked Defigns*, we find to be too true, by woful Experience ; but what then, do's that argue that it is *not to be determin'd* who has this Divine Right ? certainly no; for tho' through *Herefy* and *Schifm* the Minds of many Men are fo dreadfully blinded that they do not difcover this great Truth ; yet, God be prais'd, thofe who continue in the Communion of the *Truly Catholick* and *Apoftolick Church*, and are *Diligent* and *Inquifitive* to know God's Will, and to live according to that knowledge, need never be put to fo great a plunge, as to be in doubt and fufpenfe concerning this Difpute, or the Validity of their Baptifm; which they have receiv'd from the Lawfully ordain'd Minifters of Chrift ; becaufe fuch Minifters muft be *vifible* and *known* as long as ther is or fhall
H . be

be any Truly *Organiz'd Church* of Chrift
in the World ; and that ther fhall be *always* fuch a Church is plain by our Saviour's promife, That *the Gates of Hell fhall
not prevail againft it* ; and as for the true
Minifters therof, that they fhall alfo continue, is as certain, by his promifing thus
to his Apoftles, *Lo I am with you alway,
even unto the End of the World* ; and this
is further confirm'd by the Apoftle St.
Paul's affuring us, that when Chrift
Afcended up on High, *he gave fome Apoftles, and fome Prophets, and fome Evangelifts, and fome Paftors, and Teachers, for
the* 𝕻𝖊𝖗𝖋𝖊𝖈𝖙𝖎𝖓𝖌 *of the Saints,* &c. ——
'*till we all come into the* 𝖀𝖓𝖎𝖙𝖞 *of the
Faith,* &c. — *unto a* 𝕻𝖊𝖗𝖋𝖊𝖈𝖙 𝕸𝖆𝖓 Now
'tis certain that this *Perfection* and *entire
Unity* will not be compleated till the
End of the World, and therfore thefe
Officers appointed to bring about fuch excellent Purpofes, muft continue *fo long*
and be *vifible* among us : And that this
their continuance in the Church is to be
fo plain and *perfpicuous,* as that it fhall be
eafie to difcover and diftinguifh them
from *falfe Teachers* and *new Upftarts,* is
evident by another Defign, for which our
Lord appointed them, *viz. That we henceforth fhould be no more Children tofs'd to
and*

*and fro, and carried about with every Wind
of Doctrine by the flight of Men, and cunning Craftiness whereby they lie in wait to
deceive,* (*Eph.* 4. 14.) For how can the
Ministers of Christ defend us against every Wind of Doctrine, and the Cunning
Craftiness of *Deceivers,* if they are not
to be visible and known to us ? So that
as sure as God is true, so sure we are,
that his duly Authoriz'd and rightly Commission'd Ministers, *i. e. Apostles* and *Prophets,* &c. shall continue, and be known
by the truly Sincere, to the Consummati-
on of all things ; and therefore we shall
never want such to Administer his Holy
Sacraments, and consequently need never
be in Suspense either about their *Divine
Authority,* or the *Validity* of our Baptism
Administer'd by their Hands ; so that
my affirming Baptism to be *Invalid* for
want of such Divine Authority or Commission in the Administrator, do's not
put this Divine Institution upon an uncertain, but a *sure* and *lasting* Foundation.

BUT here I expect that it will be
ask'd in whom do I suppose this *Divine
Authority* to be fix'd ? I answer, that I do
not only suppose, but firmly and undoubt-
ingly *Believe,* after a strict and impartial

Enquiry

Enquiry which I have deliberately made into this Matter ; that 'twas settled by Christ himself at first, and *continually* convey'd down to this Day, in 𝕰𝖕𝖎𝖘𝖈𝖔𝖕𝖆𝖈𝖞 𝖔𝖓𝖑𝖞, and of this I am *as certain as that* our first Day of the Week was appointed by Christ and his Apostles, to be the *Christian Sabbath*, nay, tho' I am very well satisfy'd that this our Christian Sabbath is of Divine Appointment ; yet I can safely affirm, that the Arguments by which it is to be prov'd, are not so *numerous* as those for the Divine Right of Episcopacy ; as may easily be demonstrated whensoever it shall be put to the Trial : as for those who are of another Opinion, I wish they had either more Knowledge, or more Humility ; it is none of my Business here, to endeavour their Conviction : but if they would use their utmost Diligence to do the Will of God in all other Instances of their Duty, and seek to him for that Wisdom which is from above, enquiring without Prejudice, by attentively reading the Sacred Oracles ; and comparing therewith, what has been said by many excellent Authors upon this Subject ; I hope they would then. *know of this Doctrine whether it be of God* ; which that they

may

may I heartily recommend thefe few Modern Books to their ferious perufal, *viz.*

A Modeft Proof of the Order and Government fettled by Chrift and his Apoftles in the Church. Printed for *John Wyat,* at the *Rofe* in St. *Paul's Church-Yard,* 1705.

A Difcourfe fhewing who they are that are now qualify'd to Adminifter Baptifm and the Lord's Supper. Printed for *C. Browne,* at the *Sun* at the *Weft-End* of St. *Paul's,* 1698.

Dr. Potter *of Church Government.* Printed for *Tim. Child,* at the *White Hart* in St. *Paul's Church-Yard,* 1707.

Dr. Hickes's *two Treatifes, one of the Chriftian Priefthood, the other of the Dignity of the Epifcopal Order.* Printed for *Richard Sare,* at *Grays-Inn-Gate* in *Holborn,* 1707.

And a little Book call'd, *The Plain Man's Guide to the True Church.* Printed for *R. Clavel,* at the *Peacock* in St. *Paul's Church-Yard,* 1708.

IV. But fome it's likely will Charge me with uncharitablenefs, in denying the Va-

H 3   lidity

lidity of the Baptifms of Foreign Churches, where there is no Epifcopal Ordination; and of many Good and Pious Men
who are without fuch Ordination among
our felves.

Anf. The Main drift of my Effay is a-
gainft the Validity of that Baptifm which
Men know themfelves to have receiv'd
from Perfons who were never Divinely
Commiffion'd, and yet prefume to ufurp
this Authority in *Oppofition* to the Divine
Right of Epifcopacy : Which being duly
confider'd, frees me from Anfwering to
this Charge, with refpect to fuch Foreign
Churches, fome of which have told you
that they do not Act in *Oppofition* to Epifcopacy; and have pleaded that they lie
under a Neceffity not to have Bifhops
among them; but that they *highly* value
and reverence that Order in our *Englifh*
Church. Whether this Plea of Neceffity
be good, or whether it affects them *fo far*
as to hinder their receiving Epifcopal Ordination from other Proteftant Churches,
tho' they cannot have Bifhops refiding a-
mong themfelves, is not my Bufinefs (here)
to enquire ; but this I'm fure of, that ther
is not the leaft Reafon (nay, 'tis impi-
ous) to Complement away the Great
Truths

Truths of God, to pleaſe any, tho' never ſo great a Party of Men.

THE Divine Right of Epiſcopacy is plain from Scripture, and was never call'd in queſtion by any conſiderable Number of Men, till within theſe laſt two hundred Years; and muſt we now lay it aſide for fear of oppoſing new upſtart Notions and Opinions? God forbid! muſt our holding faſt the ſound Doctrine of Chriſt and his Apoſtles be call'd uncharitable and unkind, becauſe it do's not ſuit with the Temper and Diſpoſition of other People? Cannot we ſtill keep our Charity for them by Believing that God may diſpenſe with the very want of the Chriſtian Sacraments, and beſtow even the Supernatural Graces of them, to thoſe who labour either *under an Invincible Ignorance*, or elſe *an impoſſibility of receiving thoſe Sacraments*, when they do all that lies in their Power to fulfil his Bleſſed Will? certainly we may, for God can diſpenſe with his own Inſtitutes, and give the Spiritual Graces annex'd to them, to whom he pleaſes (by *Axiom* 2.)

BUT as for ſome of thoſe among our ſelves, I fear their Caſe is very dangerous, becauſe abundance of them ſeem to want ſo fair an Excuſe, living under that Epiſ-

H 4 copal

copal Government which they refuse to
acknowledge and submit to : but God only
knows their several Circumstances of
Knowledge and Capacity, and the Strength
of those Prejudices which some of them
may have contracted by their Education :
He is Infinite Goodness it self, and will
never punish any for what they *never
could help*. But as for the Slothful and
Negligent, the Obstinate and Perverse, we
have no Authority from Divine Revelation to hope any thing for their Advantage. But to sum up my whole Answer
to this Objection in the Words of an excellent Modern Author.

" *THOSE who have been Baptiz'd by*
" *Persons not lawfully Ordain'd, and con-*
" *sequently they have receiv'd no Baptism,*
" *having receiv'd it from those who had*
" *no Commission to Administer it, but who*
" *were guilty of the Highest Sacrilege in*
" *Usurping such a Sacred Commission, not*
" *lawfully deriv'd to them by a Successive*
" *Ordination from the Apostles :* [as is the
Case with us] " *But yet thro' a general*
" *Corruption of the Times, such Baptisms*
" *are suffer'd to pass, whereby the Persons*
" *so Baptiz'd swimming down the Stream,*
" *do think their Baptism to be Valid, and*
" *therefore seek not for a Re-baptization,* [I
                                            had

had rather ſay True Baptiſm]. " *from*
" *thoſe who are empower'd to Adminiſter*
" *it. I ſay, where no ſuch Rebaptization*
[or rather True Baptiſm] " *is taught, and*
" *therby the People know nothing of it, in*
" *ſuch Caſe their Ignorance is in a manner*
" *Invincible, and their Sincerity and De-*
" *votion in receiving no Sacraments, yet*
" *thinking them True Sacraments, may be*
" *accepted by God, and the Inward Grace*
" *conferr'd.* But this Caſe do's not reach
thoſe who do, or may know and act better, and is the whole of my Charity in
this matter, and I think a ſufficient Anſwer
to the Objection.

V. Another Objection in Defence of
the Validity of Baptiſms Adminiſter'd by
ſuch as have not the Divine Commiſſion, is the Example of *Zipporah, Moſes*'s
Wife, who Circumcis'd her Son, and therby ſaved her Husband's Life ; for God
ſought to kill *Moſes,* and when ſhe had
Circumcis'd her Son, he let him go ; and
therfore approv'd of her Act in ſo doing,
tho' ſhe had no right to do ſo by the Inſtitution.

Anſ. Whoſoever will but look into the
firſt Inſtitution of Circumciſion, will find,
That God did not ſet apart a particular
Order of Men for this purpoſe, but only
requir'd,

requir'd, *Gen.* 17. 10. *Every Man Child among you shall be Circumcis'd* ; &c. to the 15th Verse, *Every Male must be Circumcis'd* ; but the Persons who should continually Administer this Circumcision, are not Nam'd in the Institution.

Nay, tho' it should be granted that Circumcision was to be perform'd by the Master, as he was the Priest of his Family, yet it do's not follow that *Zipporah* did any thing more than what she had a right to do, because her *Husband's Authority* was devolv'd upon her in his Sickness, when he was unable to do it himself; Especially, considering that this Sickness was inflicted upon him, because his Son had not been Circumcis'd, and that he might therfore *Order* his Wife to do it in his stead ; and consequently 'twas Interpretatively done by himself, because by his Authority ; as we find in the Issue by God's sparing his Life when the Circumcision was perform'd ; and by *Zipporah's* Words to *Moses*, when she had cut off the Fore-Skin of her Son, and cast it at *his Feet*, saying, *A Bloody Husband thou art, because of the Circumcision, Exod.* 5. 25, 26. which plainly implies, that she did it for his Sake and by his Order. But what do's all this avail to those, who

know-

knowingly receive, or acquiesce in Baptism receiv'd, from such as have no *Divine Commission* ; when they may be Baptiz'd by Chrift's own Miniſters, whom he has particularly appointed *excluſive* of all others to Baptize ? This is acting even contrary to the Example here Objected, becauſe by all that can be ſeen in the Text, ſhe acted by a *Divine Commiſſion,* even by Virtue of an Immediate Revelation to *Moſes* her Husband, whom God doubtleſs acquainted with the cauſe of his Diſpleaſure, and the means of appeaſing his Anger by *this* Circumciſion of his Son ; which was *an extraordinary* and *unuſual Caſe,* and not at all parallel to the unauthoriz'd Miniſtrations of thoſe who act *in oppoſition* to that *Divine Commiſſion,* which has been Succeſſively handed down, from Chriſt and his Apoſtles in all Ages.

VI. Another Objection is a Maxim, which ſome would perſwade us will hold good in Chriſtian Baptiſm, and that is, *Fieri non debet ; factum valet.* i. e *It is not Lawful to be done, yet being done, 'tis Valid.*

Anſ. Tho' this Maxim may hold good in ſome Secular Caſes, yet it do's not therfore follow that it will ſo in all. For
Example,

Example, 'tis not Lawful for me to make a Man Free of the City of *London*, and though I should be never so serious and formal in pretending, or should really suppose my self to have sufficient Authority, to give such a Freedom, yet 'tis certain that such a Freedom given by me, would never be Valid, the Man must receive a Legal Freedom, notwithstanding the Counterfeit one he had of me : the like may be justly affirm'd of the Naturalization of Foreigners ; and many other great Concerns of this World ; and if this Maxim will not hold good in these, and abundance of other worldly things ; how much less in those of an infinitely higher Nature, in the Divine Positive Institutions, which God has made to be the Means and Pledges of *Supernatural Benefits*, to be conferr'd on us by the Ministration of *his own Particularly Commission'd and Authoriz'd Ambassadors* : Especially when we remember that this Maxim was never *appointed* by him, to be our Rule and Guide in any of our Affairs, much less in those of a Religious and Spiritual Nature, as without all doubt Christian Baptism is. Besides, the Objection acknowledges that it is *not Lawful*, therfore 'tis Sinful, and how a 𝕾𝖎𝖓𝖋𝖚𝖑

Act

Act ſhould be **valid** for **Supernatural purpoſes** is utterly inconceivable, nay, 'tis abominable to affirm it.

VII. Another Objection which I have heard of, is, That the Council of *Eliberis*, *Anno* 305, allow'd of *Lay Baptiſm* in a Caſe of neceſſity: that the Church of *Rome* do's ſo to this Day: and that the Church of *England* did ſo in the Reign of King *Edward* the Sixth; of Queen *Elizabeth*; and in the beginning of King *James* the firſt, as is plain by the ſeveral Common Prayer Books in thoſe Days; particularly King *Edward's*, *Anno* 1552, and King *James's*, 1621, ſtill to be ſeen at *Sion College* Library in *London*.

Anſ. I grant the Truth of theſe Matters of Fact, but cannot agree that thoſe Allowances were Conſonant to, but rather directly againſt, the Divine Inſtitution of this Sacrament, for the ſeveral Reaſons I have already mention'd in this Eſſay.

AS for the Council of *Eliberis*, I have cited it Page 12, of *The Preliminary Diſcourſe*, where 'tis requir'd by the Canon, That ſuch a Perſon as had receiv'd but *Lay Baptiſm* ſhould, if he liv'd, be preſented by the *Lay Man* who Baptiz'd him, to the Biſhop, to be *perfected* by Impoſition of Hands; intimating therby,

by, That such Baptism is not perfect without it. Now suppofing (but not grant-
ing) that fuch Impofition of Hands could
perfect fuch *imperfect Baptifms*, our *Lay
Baptizers* break the Canon of this Council. becaufe they Baptize *without any neceffity at all*, and being in oppofition to
their Bifhop, refufe to prefent fuch Perfons to him for the *perfecting* of their Baptifms by Impofition of his Hands, fo that
this Canon will ftand the Objector in no
ftead, till 'tis obeyed in *all its parts*;
and then 'twill have no force againft what
I have faid, till it can be prov'd that fuch
Impofition of Hands is fufficient to give
Validity to Invalid Baptifms, for all fuch
imperfect Baptifms are no better, if the
Corollary of the 3d *Propofition* be true.

AS for the Church of *Rome*, her Allowances in this Cafe are no Rule to us
Proteftants, who have feparated from her
for her many Grofs Errours, both in Doctrine and Practice ; fhe began to Quarrel
with St. *Cyprian*, and other Primitive Bifhops, and carried it very unchriftianly
againft them, for not allowing any Validity in fuch Baptifms, and has ever fince
perfifted in this ill Humour, fo far as at
laft to condemn thofe who do not believe
the Validity of Baptifm Adminifter'd by
Women,

Women, whose Authoritative Acts in the
Church of God, are both contrary to the
Law of Nature, and also forbidden by
the Holy Ghost himself. "Saint *Basil*
" in his 10th Epistle, complains of the
" Western Bishops, and particularly the
" Roman, *Quod Veritatem neque Norunt,*
" *neque discere sustinent.* ——— *Cum iis*
" *qui veritatem ipsis annuncidnt contenden-*
" *tes, hæresin autem per se ipsos stabilien-*
" *tes : That they neither know the Truth,*
" *nor care to learn it ; but they contend*
" *with them who tell them the Truth, and*
" *by themselves establish Heresie ;* for which
Reason their Authority ought not to be
objected in this Matter by a Protestant ;
especially considering that such an Objector will not submit to their Decisions,
even in things of a much more Inferior
Nature.

I confess the Practice of the Church of
England, in this Case, would have been
a formidable Objection, if she her self
had not answer'd it already by purging
her Liturgy of so Inconsistent a Rubrick :
I call it Inconsistent, because, especially in
King *James* the first's Reign, she had declar'd in her Articles of Religion, that
it is *unlawful,* i. e. *Sinful* for any Man to
Administer Sacraments until he be *Law-*
fully

fully call'd and Sent; and at the same time allow'd by her Rubrick to Private Baptism, that *any one there present* might Baptize the Infant (*in a Case of Necessity*;) and yet upon the Priest's Examination afterwards into the Lawfulness of the Child's Baptism, it was requir'd, that this Question should be put to the Persons who brought the Child to Church, *viz.* " *Whether they* " *think the Child be Lawfully and perfectly* " *Baptiz'd*, which (considering the preceeding Questions, " *whether 'twas Bap-* " *tiz'd with Water, and in the Name of* " *the Trinity*, &c.) seems to be needless and to no purpose, except by asking their Thoughts about the Lawfulness and Perfection of such a Baptism, they meant to make it *Lawful* or *Unlawful*, as the Persons they put such a Question to, should think it : Which is a very strange, and indeed a precarious and uncertain Foundation for us to build the Validity of our Baptism upon, in such a Case of Necessity. And therfore 'tis no wonder that the Church of *England*, upon a more exact Review of her Liturgy, expung'd this Question out of the Rubrick, and also for very weighty Reasons took away the Liberty of *Lay Baptizing*, in her present Liturgy, by requiring, even in Cases of
Necessity

Neceſſity, that Baptiſm ſhould be Adminiſter'd by " *The Miniſter of the Pariſh*
" *or any other Lawful Miniſter that can be*
" *procur'd* ; which is a Subſtantial Anſwer
to all Objections that may be rais'd from
her former Practice, when ſhe was but in
the Infancy of her Reformation, and not
long Emerg'd out of the thick Darkneſs
of Popiſh Errour and Superſtition. But
if ſuch a Cuſtom had been ſtill continu'd,
St *Cyprian* long ſince lay'd it down for *an*
Undoubted Truth, " *That we are not to*
" *be determin'd by any Cuſtoms of that Na-*
" *ture, but to Examine whether they will*
" *bear the teſt of Reaſon.* And Biſhop *Tay-*
lor ſays, (ſpeaking of Baptiſm by Mid-
wives) " *This Cuſtom came in at a wrong*
" *Door, it lean'd upon a falſe and Super-*
" *ſtitious Opinion ; and they thought it bet-*
" *ter to Invade the Prieſt's Office, than to*
' *truſt God with the Souls which he made*
" *with his own Hands, and Redeemed with*
" *his Son's Blood, but this Cuſtom was not*
" *to be follow'd, if it had ſtill continu'd ;*
" *for even then they confeſs'd it was Sin,*
" *Factum valet, fieri non debuit ; and Evil*
" *ought not to be done for a good end,* &c.
" *This Cuſtom therfore is of the Nature of*
" *thoſe which are to be laid aſide. No*
" *Man Baptizes but he that is in Holy Or-*
I   *ders*

" ders, said Simeon of Theſſalonica ; and
" I think he ſaid truly. But above all
" things, Opinions are not to be taken up
" by Cuſtom, and reduc'd to practice : Not
" only becauſe Cuſtom is no good warranty
" for Opinions, &c. But beſides this, when
" an Opinion is offer'd only by the hand of
" Cuſtom, it is commonly a Sign of a Bad
" Cauſe, and that ther is nothing elſe to be
" ſaid for it, Ductor Dubitantium, fourth
" Edition, Page 638, 639.

AND in the ſame Book, Page 198,
" In all Moral Actions, ther muſt be a Sub-
" ſtantial Poteſtative Principle that muſt
" have proportion'd Power to the Effect ;
" a thing cannot be done without a Cauſe,
" and Principle in Morality, any more than
" in Nature. If a Woman goes about to
" Conſecrate the Holy Sacrament, it is an
" ineffective Hand, ſhe Sins for attempt-
" ing it ; and cannot do it afterwards ; and
" it were wiſer and truer, if Men will
" think the ſame thing of their giving Bap-
" tiſm, unleſs they will confeſs that to Bap-
" tize Children is a mere Natural and Se-
" cular Action, to which Natural Powers
" are ſufficient ; or that Women have re-
" ceiv'd Spiritual Powers to do it, and that
" whether a Prieſt or a Woman do's it, it
" no difference, but matter of Order only
                                        " If

" *If an effect be Spiritual, the Agent muſt be*
" *ſo too* ; thus far that Great Biſhop : And
if his Reaſons are good againſt Womens
Baptizing, as I think they are, they will
be as good to all Intents and Purpoſes a-
gainſt a Man's preſuming to do the like
without the *Divine Commiſſion* : becauſe,
he is equally deſtitute of a Spiritual Power, and *in fact* is as little in Holy Orders
as ſhe.

VIII. The laſt Objection that I ſhall
mention is, what ſome great Men have
made uſe of, to Eſtabliſh the Validity of
Lay Baptiſm ; and that is, That tho' it
was a Sin for the Two Hundred and Fifty
Princes to offer Incenſe ; yet by even that
Sinful offering the Cenſers, wherewith
they offer'd *were hallow'd,* and God himſelf declared them to be ſo, *Numbers* 16.
in like manner, tho' it be a Sin for *Laymen*
to Baptize; yet the Perſon ſo Baptiz'd is
therby Hallow'd and Sanctify'd ; and conſequently ſuch a Baptiſm is Valid.

Anſ. This Objection has no manner of
Force for the purpoſe deſign'd, becauſe
'tis not in the leaſt parallel to Chriſtian
Baptiſm ; for the Cenſers (mere ſenſeleſs
things) were Capable of no *Supernatural
Spiritual Graces and Priviledges* to be *en-*
joy'd by them, by virtue of that Offering ;

but

but the Objects of Baptism, Sensible, Ra
tional, and Immortal Souls, are to be pof
fefs'd of, and to be made happy by, such
unspeakable Benefits and Advantages as
are annex'd to Baptism. The Censers
were wholly Passive; but the Baptiz'd
Person is not so, for even in Infancy he
is Active by his Sponsors, (and when he
comes to Years, must be so in his own
Person The Censers, tho' they were hallow'd, yet they were not hallow'd to the
same purpose, as the Censers wherewith
Aaron offer'd Incense; for God did not
order those Two Hundred and Fifty Cen-
fer to be continu'd, for the *same use* to
which those Sinners put them, but requir'd
them *to be made broad Plates for a Covering
of the Altar : To be a Memorial unto the
Children of* Israel, *that no Stranger which
is not of the Seed of* Aaron *come near to offer
Incense before the Lord*, (Num. 16. 39, 40.)
So that it these Censers are a Parallel Inftance for Persons Baptiz'd by *uncommissi-
on'd* pretenders, then the use that God
order'd them to be put to, should teach
us to make the like use of such Sinfully
Baptiz'd Persons, *viz.* To make them Memorials to all Chriftians that none who are
not Commission'd by Chrift, should dare to
come near to Baptize in the Christian
Church:

Church : But how fhall fuch finfully Baptiz'd Perfons become fuch Memorials fo effectually, as by renouncing their falfe, and receiving true Chriftian Baptifm from Chrift's Authoriz'd Minifters, and therby fruftrate as much as they can, the prefumptuous *Ufurpations* of thofe who have no Divine Miffion for fo great a Miniftration ? This is the moft proper inference that can be drawn from thefe Cenfers, with refpect to fuch as are unlawfully Baptiz'd : Tho' after all, they have nothing in them that can with any Coherence, be juftly adapted to the Inftitution of Chriftian Baptifm, or any one Effential Part therof : The Two Hundred and Fifty Princes, indeed, if compar'd to the Unauthoriz'd Adminiftrators of Baptifm may be fomething to the purpofe ; and fo may the Incenfe if compared to the Water in Baptifm ; becaufe, as this when rightly Adminifter'd, is the means of Spiritual Benefits, fo Incenfe, when rightly offer'd *i. e.* by a Divinely Commiffion'd Perfon, was a means likewife of procuring the favour of God, by making an Atonement for the Sins of the People. But as for the Cenfers, they were *only* the Veffels wherein this Incenfe, the outward Means of the Attonement, was contain'd ; fo that they

I 3   have

have not the least reference, either to the Person Administring, or the Water of Baptism, or to the Person Baptized ; and therfore, if the Objector will have them to be Parallel to any thing at all in this matter, they must be so to the Vessel which contains the Baptism Water : And he may make as much use as he pleases of that Parallelism, which is nothing at all to our present purpose.

UPON the whole, the Grand Design of these Princes was (in opposition to the Establish'd Priesthood) to offer Incense before the Lord, *contrary to a Divine Positive Institution, which confin'd that Action to* Aaron *and his Sons only ;* This Offering being thus unlawful, for want of the Divine Authority of the Persons Administring, was so far from being accepted, that it was a crying Abomination ; and instead of procuring a Blessing, either for themselves or their Abettors, drew down upon them swift Destruction ; the Princes being immediately consum'd by a Fire from the Lord, and Fourteen Thousand Seven Hundred of their Partizans destroy'd by a Plague. Even so, if any thing about Baptism may be hence infer'd, we may justly fear that the Administration of suppos'd Baptism by Un-

commission'd

commiffion'd Perfons, in Oppofitioh to the Divinely eftablifh'd Priefthood of the Chriftian Church, inftead of being a Means of conveying Spiritual Graces and Bene-fits, to thofe who *knowingly* receive, or acquiefce in it, will rather exclude both fuch Giver and Receiver, (tho' they efcape God's Judgments here) from the infinite Priviledges of his Children hereafter, with-out a fincere and fpeedy Repentance.

Some other Objections I have endea-vour'd to obviate in the Progrefs of this Effay, and therfore fhall only further De-clare, that I fincerely believe the Subject of this Difcourfe to be a Subftantial Truth; nay, even a firft Principle of Chriftiani-ty, and that without the couragious Af-ferting and Vindication therof, the whole Chriftian Priefthood and the Divine Au-thority of it, muft be call'd in queftion, (as we fee it has lately been in Publick Print) and confequently in time fo far deny'd, as to Incourage every bold Intru-der to ufurp that Sacred Office and Mini-ftry, even in oppofition to that Divine Commiffion, which has been conftantly handed down from Chrift and his Apo-ftles, to this very Day.

I hope therfore that *None who are vefted with this Divine Authority*, will fight a-

I 4   gainft

gainst *it* by appearing publickly in opposition to the Subject of this Essay : as for
my manner of Arguing to defend it, ther
may be some *undesign'd Faults* in it, which
I humbly submit to their just Correction,
and prudent Censure ; hoping they will
execute *both*, with so much Wisdom and
Conduct, as (to make me see my own
Errours, and at the same time) not to
prejudice, but add Strength and Cogency
to the Cause I have pleaded, which ought
by no means to suffer for my *Weakness* in
its Defence.

AS for the mere Pretenders to this Divine Authority, I have nothing to say to
them or their Followers ; but only to desire 'em to take care not to deceive themselves, but seriously to enquire whether
ther is any Legality in that Commission,
by which they Act ; which till they can
solidly prove, I shall always esteem to be
utterly Invalid for the Administration of
Christian Sacraments. I shall not trouble
my self to enter the Lists with them, tho'
they quarrel never so much with what I
have said ; they have Work enough already cut out to their Hands, in those excellent Books which I have mention'd in my
Answer to the 3d Objection ; and to
                                        their

their Arguments, I refer them for the **Divine Right of Episcopacy** that they may ſave themſelves the trouble of demanding them from me.

I F they ſhall oppoſe my aſſertion of the Neceſſity of a Divine Commiſſion to Adminiſter Baptiſm, they will thereby *Confound* themſelves when they affirm that they Baptize by Virtue of ſuch a Commiſſion : And then I ſhall not think them worth my Anſwering.

I conclude all with my hearty Prayers to Almighty God, that this my weak endeavour may be for his Glory, and *that he would keep us from all* **Falſe Doctrine, Hereſie and Schiſm**; *that all who profeſs and call themſelv's Chriſtians may be led into the* **Way of Truth,** *and hold the Faith in Unity of Spirit, in the Bond of Peace, and in Righteouſneſs of Life*; *and that he would be pleas'd to Illuminate* **All Biſhops, Prieſts and Deacons,** *with true Knowledge and Underſtanding of his Word, that both by their Preaching and Living, they may ſet it forth and ſhew it accordingly*: *and rightly and duly Adminiſter* **His Holy Sacaments,** *that ſo* **Jeroboams Prieſts** *may not* **Prophane His Service,** *but that* **The Seed of Aaron** *may ſtill* **Miniſter** *before him*; *to whom with*

with his Eternal Son, and Holy Spirit, Three Persons, but One God, be ascrib'd, as is most due, All Honour, Praise, and Glory, Might, Majesty and Dominion, by every Creature that is in Heaven and Earth, and under the Earth, For ever and ever, Amen.

A P-

APPENDIX.

SINCE the Publication of the First
Edition of this Book, I am inform'd,
that some Gentlemen of no mean Character, have made further Objections a-
gainst the Subject therof, which (because
they look very plausible at first sight, and
may therfore prejudice too many. against
what I have propos'd) I shall endeavour
here to answer, as briefly and plainly as
I can.

Obj. IX. AND First 'tis said, that if Lay
Baptism be Invalid, and the Divine Commission to Baptize be convey'd from the
Apostles in Episcopacy only, then all those
Foreign Reform'd Churches which have
no Episcopal Ordination are effectually
Unchurch'd, as being (by the Principles asserted by me) destitute of a
Christian Ministry, and consequently of
Christian Baptism, which is a consequence
so dreadful, and even contrary to the Concessions of many Episcopal Divines of the
Church of *England*, that none ought to
admit of that Doctrine, from which (if
granted) so great a mischief must necef-
sarily arise. *Anſw.*

Anſw. That Lay Baptiſm is Null and Void, I humbly conceive, I have prov'd; if not, let the Authors of this Objection ſhew, either the Inſufficiency, or Fallacy of the Arguments I have produc'd for that purpoſe; otherwiſe I ſhall take it for granted, that they acknowledge ſuch Baptiſms to be Invalid; or elſe, that at beſt they can give no ſolid Reaſons for their Validity. And therfore, till I hear further from them upon this ſingle Topick, I ſhall give my ſelf no more trouble about it, but proceed to the conveyance of the Divine Commiſſion to Baptize, and this (ſuppoſing Lay Baptiſm to be Invalid) can be convey'd from the Apoſtles in the Chriſtian Miniſtry only; ſo that all our Buſineſs here, is to know how the Chriſtian Miniſtry was handed down, and ſucceſſively continued from the Apoſtles to our Days, and this will determine who can Adminiſter Valid Baptiſm.

THAT the Chriſtian Miniſtry was conveyed from the Apoſtles in Epiſcopacy only, we have a Cloud of Witneſſes; Firſt, the Practice of the Apoſtles, recorded in the Sacred Oracles of infallible Truth the Holy Scriptures; Secondly, all Eccleſiaſtical Hiſtory; and Thirdly, the conſtant and uninterrupted Practice of the
Univerſal

Universal Church of Chrift in all Ages and Places, for One Thoufand Five Hundred Years together fiom the Apoftles Days. Thefe all bear teftimony to this great Truth, as has been fufficiently demonftrated by a vaft number of the beft Chriftian Writers, particularly fome of our own Nation, and that very lately, (*vid. Thofe I have mention'd in Anfwer to the 3d Ob ection, and another Entituled,* The Divine Right of Epifcopacy, *Printed for Richard Sare, at Grays-Inn-Gate in Holborn,* 1708,) who have obviated and anfwer'd the Objections of all Enemies fo excellently well, that it would be no lefs than Prefumption in me, to attempt to fay any thing more upon that Subject, after fuch Learned Authors ; to whom therfore I refer the Reader for his fatisfaction in this Point, and pafs on to confider the Objection it felf.

IF then the Premifes above mention'd be true ; If Lay Baptifm be Invalid, *&c.* then (fays the Objector) " *all thofe Foreign* " *Reform'd Churches,* &c. *are effectually Un-* " *church'd, being deftitute of a Chriftian Mi-* " *niftry, and confequently of Chriftian Bap-* " *tifm.* Why truly, if thofe Foreign Reform'd are Unchurch'd upon the truth of thofe Premifes, I cannot help that, 'tis the

Objector

Objector himself that tells me they are so; and I know of no way for him to help them out of that Difficulty at present, but either to prove the Premises false; or else to perswade them to receive Episcopal Ordination. But 'tis said, " *this is a dread-* " *ful consequence* : It may be so, and very dreadful too, if they are so far Unchurch'd as to be reduc'd to a state of absolute Infidels, which I hope the Objector does not mean when he says they are Unchurch'd, if he does, I must tell him, that (tho' I am no Latitudinarian) I have more charitable Thoughts concerning Thousands of them than he has, upon the supposition of their being destitute of Christian Baptism: for I believe abundance of them may be included in the Number of those, whom I have spoke of in the Words of a most Excellent modern Author, (*towards the End of my Answer to the Fourth Objection*) and that therfore they may very fairly be esteem'd **as much in the Church** as the Catechumeni, or Candidates for Christian Baptism, were us'd to be in the Primitive times. This I think abates much of the dreadfulness of the Consequence to the Honest and Sincere; but it cannot be hence infer'd, that their Ministry and Ministrations are Good and Valid, or that

those

thofe who know their Defects fhould concur and communicate with 'em in fuch
their Deviations from the Divine Inftitutes.

BUT (to proceed) this fays the Ob-
jector, is "*even contrary to the Conceffions of*
"*many Epifcopal Divines of the Church of*
" England. I fuppofe he means fome of the
Writers fince the Reformation, who have
endeavour'd to make Excufes and Salvo's
for the Prefbyterian and Lay Ordinations
abroad. In reference to whom I muft
needs fay, that 'tis juftly to be fear'd, they
have done more hurt by fuch their Conceffions, than at the time of their writing
them they were aware of; for 'tis not to
be doubted, that many put a great value
upon the Judgment of fuch Learned and
Good Men, and therby have been induc'd
to believe that fuch Ordinations are Good
and Valid, and confequently that ther's no
need for thofe Foreign Reformed to feek
for Epifcopal Ordination, wherby too
many of the Foreign Teachers themfelves,
are inftead of being cur'd of, confirm'd
in their Errors, and it may be hinder'd
from fo much, as but enquiring whether
they are in the right or no. With fubmiffion to better Judgments, fuch large
Conceffions of thofe *many Epifcopal Divines,*
have

have been not only Prejudicial and Hurtful
to the Reform'd abroad, but even contrary
to the Doctrine and avow'd Practice of
the Church of *England*, which they were
oblig'd in conscience by their Subscription,
to support and maintain.　For, does she
not teach in her 23. Article, that "*It is not*
"*lawful* (therfore 'tis sinful and contrary to
their Institution) "*for any Man to take up-*
"*on him the Office of Ministring the Sacra-*
"*ments before he be lawfully Call'd and Sent?*
And does she not confine this **lawful Call-**
ing and Sending to **Episcopal Ordi-**
nation, in the Preface to her Form and
Manner of Making, Ordaining, and Consecrating of Bishops, Priests and Deacons?
Does she not call this **Episcopal Ordina-**
tion, Christ's Commission and Autho-
rity, when in her 26th Article she teaches,
that the Minister when he Administers the
Sacraments does it "*in Christ's Name, and*
"*by his Commission and Authority?*　Is she
not so exactly consistent to all this, that she
will not admit any of these Foreign Teachers into the Number of her Priests, no nor
of her Deacons neither, without Episcopal Ordination?　Is not all this so true that
none can deny it?　And does she not therby, as much as may be, prevent all such
Concessions, and reprove those who make
them,

them, contrary to her Doctrine and Practice? I think she does, and confequently that her Articles, are not of so loose and variable a Contexture as some (who ought to know better) have reprefented them to. be, (like a Nofe of Wax) that may be wrefted to ferve any turn, and defend almoft all Contradictious Doctrines and Practices whatfoever, without confidering that her Articles, Rubricks, and Canons, &c. when duly compar'd with one another, do make the moft perfect Harmony and Agreement, and have nothing in them that is either Contradictory or Inconfiftent to themfelves, or difagreeable to the Holy Scriptures, and Practice of the Primitive Church.

I F in the Days of *Jeroboam* the Son of *Nebat, who made* Ifrael *to Sin,* a Prieft of the Tribe of *Aaron* fhould have undertaken to defend the Validity of the Priefthood, which *Jeroboam* had fet up, would he not have been juftly cenfurable, would he not have acted contrary to the Principles of the true Church of the *Jews* at *Jerufalem*? Certainly he would, notwithstanding the vaftly fuperior Numbers in the Ten Tribes who forfook the true Priefts, and the fmallnefs of the Numbers in the Two other Tribes, who would not *follow that*

K *Multitude*

Multitude to do this Evil. And the reason why he would have been juftly blameable is evident, becaufe *Jeroboam made Priefts of the Loweft of the People which were not of the Sons of* Levi, 1 Kings 12. 31. For that this (as well as their Idolatry) was his and the Ten Tribes Sin is evident by *Abijah's* fpeech to them, (2 *Chron.* 13. 9, 10) *Have ye not caft out the Priefts of the Lord, the Sons of* Aaron *and the* Levites, *and have made you Priefts after the manner of the Nations of other Lands,* &c. *But as for us* (i. e. the Members of the true Church of God, the other Two Tribes of *Ifrael*) *The lord is our God,* &c. *and the Priefts which Minifter unto the Lord are the Sons of* Aaron, *and the* Levites *wait upon their Bufinefs.* Here you fee that *Abijah* Triumphs and Glories in the true Priefthood with them, becaufe 'twas that which God himfelf appointed ; and he upbraids the Ten Tribes for their having fet up other Priefts, without any regard to the Divine Inftitution of the Priefthood ; their mighty Numbers, and the feeming neceffity of their being forc'd thereto by the Secular Power, was no Argument for him to allow of their Priefthood. How much lefs ought thofe Writers among us, to have ftudied fo induftrioufly, as fome of them have

have done, to prove the Validity of their Miniſtry, who are not one tenth of the preſent Univerſal Church, and who differ from them and the whole Church throughout all Ages, in not requiring their Miniſters to be Veſted with the Divine Authority by Epiſcopal Ordination.

I AM well aware of what is pleaded by thoſe *Epiſcopal Divines, viz.* That theſe Foreign Reform'd were under a Caſe of Neceſſity, and ſome of them ſay, they are ſo ſtill. But I am not yet ſatisfied what they mean by this Caſe of Neceſſity; The Church of *England,* wherof thoſe Epiſcopal Divines are Members, has not declar'd it: the Scripture is wholly ſilent about it, and on the contrary, has recorded the dreadful Puniſhments inflicted upon ſome, who to all appearance had a great deal of Reaſon to plead, that they were under great Circumſtances of Neceſſity, to aſſume to themſelves thoſe Offices, wherein they miniſtred contrary to the Divine Inſtitutions; as in the Caſes of *Saul,* 1 *Sam.* 13. from *verſe* 8. to *verſe* 14. and *Uzzah,* 2 *Sam.* 6. 6, 7. So that I am utterly at a Loſs to know, how thoſe Writers could diſcover any Caſe of Neceſſity, that *of it ſelf* was ſufficient to Authorize Men, to take upon them the Great Office

K 2   of

of mediating between God and Man. Ther is not one Inſtance (that I know of) in all the ſacred Oracles, of any one's being inſtated into ſuch an Office, even in the greateſt Caſes of Neceſſity, without an explicit Revelation of God's Will, that the Man ſhould act therin, when the ordinary appointed means of giving him his Commiſſion was wanting. And if the Excuſers of thoſe Foreign Ordinations can ſhew me ſuch an Inſtance, I ſhall be very much oblig'd to them if they will be pleas'd to do it.

NAY further, ſuppoſing that 'twere poſſible to determine a Caſe of Neceſſity, that might be ſufficient to empower Men to Adminiſter Valid Sacraments, without receiving a Commiſſion for ſo doing, by God's appointed means of Epiſcopal Or-dination, yet I dont find that any of the aboveſaid Writers have proved by good Arguments, that the ſaid Foreigners were ever under ſuch a Caſe of Neceſſity, *much leſs that they are ſo now*; and till this is prov'd, I ſee no reaſon to be at all con-cluded by the Writings of even the beſt of Men, who are not guided in their Dictates by the infallible Spirit of Truth, as the Bleſſed Apoſtles and Prophets were.

I

I KNOW that some do beg the Question, by supposing, "What if the Epis-
"copal Order were utterly Extinct, and
"no Bishops could be found to confer
"Holy Orders; must ther be no Mini-
"sters therfore in the Christian Church?
"and must the Visible Church of Christ
"cease to have a Being as such in the
"World? This at first proposing looks
to be a very weighty Question, but when
we justly reflect on the Divine Veracity
which has infallibly assur'd us, *that Christ
will be with his Apostles,* (i. e. *them and their
Successors, the Bishops,*) *alway even unto
the End of the World*; and that *the
Gates of Hell shall never prevail against the
Church*; then the Impertinence and Fol-
ly of this [*What if*] does immediately dis-
cover it self, because it supposes, what in
fact never was, nor ever will be, and therfore needs no answering because not to be
granted. But alas! supposing that it were
(as it is not) possible, for the Church to
be universally depriv'd of her Spiritual Fathers the Bishops, 'tis our Duty as well as
Safety, rather to wait and hope for, some
New Revelation of his Will for another
Institution of Men to succeed in the Christian Priesthood, than to take it upon our
selves, by such Ways and Means as he has

K 3

not

not hitherto appointed, and which will *therfore* prove ineffectual for the *fuperna-tural* Purposes of his own Divine Inftitu-tions; (becaufe 𝕸𝖆𝖓 by his own Autho-rity only, can never make a Human equal to a Divine Inftitution) but this Cafe has never happen'd yet, and therfore, no So-ciety of Men either paft or prefent, can be at all excus'd upon this fuppos'd Foun-dation.

A N D now to conclude, all that I have to fay to this Objection, no Doctrine what-foever can be prov'd to be falfe, by the Mifchiefs of thofe Confequences which neceffarily arife from it, when thofe Con-fequences themfelves are not contradictory to fome *previous Truths*; and when Men by either their wilful Sins, or fupine Neg-lects, are *the only caufes* of the Mifchiefs of thofe Confequences, for which Truth and its Affertors are no ways anfwerable. This I believe is a Maxim that will ftand the Teft of a ftrict Examination, and hold good in the Cafe before us: And I pray God to touch the Hearts of thofe who are concern'd in it, with a due fenfe of their Deviations from his Holy Inftitutes, that they may compleat *a thorow Reformation*; that the Chriftian Priefthood may recover its Antient Spiritual Glory; and that we

may

may be all bless'd with the Happiness of a Universal Communion of Saints here in the Church Militant, so as to be intituled to an entire and eternal Union and Communion with the Church triumphant in the Kingdom of Heaven.

Obj. X. 'Tis further Objected; that if Lay Baptism be Invalid, then all those who never receiv'd any other Baptism are uncapable of Holy Orders, having never been Baptiz'd; and therfore the Orders of several Episcopally Ordained Persons among us are Null and Void, and consequently so are all their Ministerial Acts too, because they never receiv'd any other than Lay Baptism. This will involve the Church into the utmost confusion; and therfore the Invalidity of Lay Baptism ought not to be allow'd by any, who value the Order and Peace of the Church.

Answ. THIS Objection raises a Consequence from an uncertain, and it may be a false Foundation; for it takes for granted, that the Incapacity of a Person to receive Holy Orders, by reason of his being Unbaptiz'd, renders Holy Orders, if confer'd on him, Null and Void; or in short, that *want of Baptism Nulls Holy Orders in any Person Ordain'd to the Ministry.* This Assertion does not yet appear

K 4 easie,

eafie, if at all to be prov'd, for thefe following Reafons.

1*ft.* Becaufe ther is a vaft difference between a Perfonal Capacity or Qualification, and an Authoritative One. For, a *Perfonal Qualification,* for the Miniftry, is, what a Man is bound to be endow'd with, **in Common** with all other Chriftians, whether he be ordain'd to the Miniftry or no, and therfore Baptifm and Holinefs of Life being equally incumbent on all Chriftians, Minifters as well as Lay-Men, may *juftly* be diftinguifh'd by the Name of *Perfonal Qualifications.*

BUT an *Authoritative Qualification* for the Miniftry is that only, wherby a Man is *feparated* and *diftinguifh'd* from the reft of Mankind, and therby empower'd to *Perfonate* and *Reprefent* the Divine Prefence, for the conveyance of Spiritual and Supernatural Benefits to us. This is what we call the Divine Commiffion, convey'd from the Apoftles in Epifcopacy, and given to the Ordain'd Perfon by Impofition of the Bifhop's Hands.

2*dly,* A PERSONAL *Qualification* may be, and in fact often is *manting,* when *an Authoritative One* remains Good and Valid; and ther's abundance of Reafon that it fhould be fo, becaufe, the *Perfonal Qualif-*

Qualification chiefly respects the Man himself, who is, or ought to be, possess'd of it, since he only will reap the benefit of having, or find the misery of being destitute of it. But the *Authoritative Qualification* as such, relates only to God, and the People ; to God, as the Minister is to be his *Proxy* and *Representative* ; and to the People as they are to receive from God the Supernatural Benefits of his *Proxy*'s Ministrations. The People receive no more advantage from the Personal Qualification of God's Representative, than they do mischief from his *Personal Immoralities*; that is, none at all, because they are neither answerable for the one or the other : if he be destitute of any such Qualifications, let him look to that, 'tis none of their business with respect to the Efficacy of his Ministrations : all that they are bound to take care of, is, that he be **truly Sent**, and if they are but once secure of that, then in all his Ministrations they are not to suppose him, but Christ himself (*whom he Personates*) to be Administring to them ; for, all Sacraments *on the Part of the Administration* are Good and Valid, only upon this **One Foundation**, without this, of Christ the Great High Priest's Administring, either

himself

himself in Perſon or by his Proxy, all Chriſtian Sacraments muſt fall to the Ground, and be of no uſe or advantage to Mankind; and therfore if we can but ſolidly, *i. e.* upon good foundation, believe, that *he* does thus Adminiſter to us, we need never concern our ſelves with the *Perſonal Qualifications* of his Repreſentative, for the Validity of thoſe Adminiſtrations, which receive their whole Efficacy from the *Authoritative Qualifications* of Chriſt himſelf, who has promis'd to make good and confirm them when perform'd by *one whom he has ſent.*

TO Exemplify all this in the Caſe before us; Holineſs of Life is Requir'd as a Perſonal Qualification, Previous to Holy Orders: this is evident from St. *Paul*'s Epiſtles to *Timothy* and *Titus*; and yet 'tis well known, that our Lord himſelf choſe *Judas Iſcariot*, a covetous Thief, and one whom he himſelf branded with the Name of *a Devil*; I ſay, 'tis well known, that he choſe this wicked Wretch to be no leſs than *an Apoſtle,* and ſent *him* to Preach and Baptize, to caſt out Devils, and to heal the Sick, as well as the reſt of the Apoſtles; for which reaſon, all his Miniſterial Acts were Good and Valid, notwithſtanding his being deſtitute of the *Perſonal Qualificati-*
on

on *of Holiness of Life*; and 'tis *universally* acknowledg'd, that the same is true of all other wicked Bishops, Priests, and Deacons whatsoever, otherwise, we could never be satisfied with the Validity of Ordinations in any *Age of Christianity*. And therfore, tho' Holiness of Life is a *necessary Personal Qualification* for the Ministry, because of great Edification to the People, *&c.* yet if a truly Ordained Minister should be a wicked Man, the People ought not to suspect the Validity of his Ministrations by reason of the wickedness of his Life, because, 'tis Christ that Administers by him as *his Proxy only*, and Christ's Ministrations are certainly Good and Valid; let his visible Representative be never so wicked, he himself (and not the People) must answer for that. This is exactly agreeable to the 26th Article of the Church of *England*, and therfore ther is no need longer to insist upon it, but to proceed to Baptism, another *Personal Qualification* for Holy Orders.

I T is certainly the indispensable Duty of *Every Minister* to be Baptiz'd, as well as to be personally Holy, because 'tis a Divine Law to which all ought to pay Obedience. For which reason I cannot omit commending the laudable Custom of
the

the Church of *Rome*, who, (tho' Corrupt and Scandalously wicked in other Matters, yet) requires her Candidates for Holy Orders to prove their Baptism, before they can be admitted into the Ministry : and I should heartily rejoyce to see the Governours of our Church require the same of her Candidates for the Ministerial Function, who, 'tis to be fear'd, ever since the Reformation, have never been enjoyn'd to bring Certificates of their Baptism, as well as of their good Behaviour and Christian Conversation. This Omission, I charitably believe, proceeded only from an Opinion, *that none would presume to enter into Holy Orders before they were Baptiz'd, and that therfore 'twas needless to require a Proof of their Baptism* : But however, if this Custom had been preserv'd, 'tis reasonable to believe, that our Ministers would (some of them) have been more strict in keeping their *Parish Registers* of Persons Baptiz'd by Lawfully Ordain'd Ministers, and not have suffer'd Schismatical *Lay Baptisms* to have been Register'd among the *True Baptisms*, as 'tis now scandalously practic'd in some Places, to the great grief of many, and I hope almost all our Divines, who have constantly oppos'd all such *unwarrantable Practices*, and will (to their Praise be it spoken)

spoken) never suffer such *Registers* to be made in their Parish Books. I say, if this good Custom of requiring Certificates of their Baptism had been continued, 'tis very likely, that no Lay Baptiz'd Person would have got such a Certificate, from the Minister of any Parish; because such a Minister's giving such a Certificate, would have been a publishing of his own fault, in making such a Register as is contrary to the Laws and Customs of the Church; for he must have mention'd the Lay-man's Name, who was said to have Baptiz'd the Person, and therby have declar'd, that he himself took part with *Schismaticks*, and consequently must have incurr'd the Penalties of the 10*th and* 57*th Canons of the Church of England*; and this might have been an effectual means of preserving our Registers entire, and consequently of keeping out of the Ministry, those who receiv'd Baptism from Lay Preachers; no other Lay-men being at least now so presumptuous, as once to pretend to Baptize. But this only by way of Digression.

A N D now to return, Christian Baptism is certainly *a Personal Qualification* for Holy Orders; and that it is no more than a *Personal One*, I infer from hence, because all Christians are **equally** bound to
be

be Baptiz'd, Minifters as well as People;
and it cannot be prov'd, that it is more the
duty of the one than of the other to be Baptiz'd: if it be faid yes it is, becaufe ther
muft of neceffity be a Chriftian Minifter,
before ther can be a Baptiz'd Lay-man;
this is not deny'd; it is certainly true ther
muft be fo; but it does not therfore follow
that he is not a Chriftian Minifter if he is
Unbaptiz'd; for 'tis not his Baptifm, but
the Commiffion that makes him a Chriftian Minifter, *or one fet apart to Minifter
in the Divine Offices of the Chriftian Religion.* If it be objected, that while he is
Unbaptiz'd he is out of the Church; and
how can he who is not of the Church, admit another by Baptifm into the Church?
I anfwer, tho' he is out of the Church
with refpect to any Benefits to himfelf, yet
not with refpect to the Spiritual Benefits,
he has Authority and Commiffion *medate-
ly* to convey to others; for, a Man may
be *a True Meffenger* to carry that Good to
another, which he himfelf neither does
nor ever will enjoy; and therfore, he who
is not of the Church becaufe Unbaptiz'd,
may *as truly* admit a Perfon into the Church
by Baptifm, as he who (tho' Baptiz'd) thro'
his Wickednefs, is deftitute of the Holy
Ghoft, can convey the Gift of the Holy
　　　　　　　　　　　　　　　　Ghoft

Ghoſt by his Miniſtration of Sacraments to others: for, as 'tis not the *Perſonal Holineſs* of the Adminiſtrator, that conveys Holineſs to me in the Miniſtration of any Sacrament; ſo neither, does his having *recciv'd* that Sacrament, ſignifie any thing to me for the Validity therof, when he Adminiſters it to me *by virtue of a Divine Commiſſion explicitly given to him.* This **Commiſſion alone**, is that which makes the Miniſtration not his, but God's own Act, and as ſuch (*without any other Appendant Cauſe*) 'tis Good and Valid. Hence our Bleſſed Lord call'd both Unbaptiz'd and Unholy Men, *viz.* his Apoſtles, who cannot be prov'd to *have been Baptiz'd in the Name of the Trinity* before his Reſurrection; and one of them, *Judas Iſcariot,* a Thief, a Devil in his Diſpoſition, to the Adminiſtration of Holy Things, as if he would therby teach us, to look with Faith on **his Authority only**, without confiding in any of the beſt Accompliſhments of thoſe on whom he has confer'd it. And if we do but look back to the Condition of the Jewiſh Church, during their forty Years ſojourning in the Wildernefs, we ſhall find that none of them were Circumcis'd in all that ſpace of time; and tho' the Uncircumcis'd was by God's own Appointment

pointment *to be cut off from among his People*, yet the Miniſtry of thoſe Prieſts and Levites, who were born in the term of thoſe Forty Years, was not Null'd and madeVoid for their want of Circumciſion; which doubtleſs was as much neceſſary to qualify them for Holy Orders, as Baptiſm is now to qualify our Chriſtian Prieſts.

UPON the whole, as neither the *Baptiſm*, nor *Perſonal Holineſs* of the Miniſter can *Baptize* or make us *Holy*, but **the Divine Authority** reſiding in him; ſo neither, can the *Baptiſm* or *Perſonal Holineſs* of the Biſhop confer Holy Orders, but **the Divine Authority** from Chriſt and his Apoſtles, viſibly convey'd to and reſiding in him : 'tis by virtue of **this alone** that Holy Orders are given, and if either the Biſhop or Ordain'd Perſon, or both, have any *Perſonal Incapacity, viz.* of Wickedneſs or want of Baptiſm, the Fault is their own, and they muſt anſwer for it ; but as for the Ordination, that muſt remain Good and Valid, by reaſon of the External Divine Commiſſion *de facto* given to the Biſhop. For, if every *Perſonal Defect* of what is requir'd, either in the Adminiſtrator or Recipient, could Invalidate the Adminiſtration, either of Baptiſm or Holy Orders, we ſhould never have an end

End of Rebaptizations and Reordinations : Nay, we could never have any certainty, either of Valid Baptifms or Ordinations, becaufe we fhould always find but too many Occafions, to call in queftion the Sufficiency of the Preparations, and Perfonal Qualifications of both Minifters and People, who are all equally expos'd to the fame Human Frailties, and lyable to be try'd with the fame innumerable Temptations.

A N D therfore I humbly conceive, our beft way is (I don't fay *only* but) **chiefly** to regard, and infift on the Vifible Divine Authority and Commiffion, handed down from Chrift and his Apoftles, by that **Order** of Men, who have *always* had power to convey it to others; this, with the *Right Matter*, and *Form* of Adminiftration, are what we ought to efteem to be the *only Effentials* of Baptifm and Ordination, on the part of the Adminiftration of them; and as for the reft, every one in particular muft do his part to the utmoft of his *Power*, to fecure thofe Perfonal Qualifications, which God has requir'd of both Minifter and People, under no lefs penalty than that of Eternal Damnation, upon the wilful neglect of them.

L   T H U S

'T H U S far I have prefum'd to declare my Thoughts, concerning the Uncertainty and (as far as I can fee) the Falfenefs of the Foundation, upon which this whole Objection is rais'd, humbly fubmitting all I have faid in oppofition to it, to the better Reafons and Arguments of my Superiors, the truly Ordain'd Minifters of Jefus Chrift, whether Bifhops, Priefts, or Deacons, fincerely declaring, that if any thing has drop'd from me, that is contrary to the Truth of Chriftianity, I do hereby Recant it, and will do fo in a more particular manner, as foon as I can difcover my Errour

A N D now, whether what I have faid againft Ordinations, and Holy Miniftrations being Null'd for want of Baptifm, be true or no, if the Invalidity of Lay Baptifm be a Truth, let every one take care to keep himfelf from the mifchievous Confequences of it. And if the Nulling of Holy Orders, and Miniftrations, be a *real Confequence* of this Truth, then ther's no other Remedy, but that thofe who are involv'd in it, fhould extricate themfelves out of it, *by Epifcopal Baptifm* and *Reordination.* It is not enough to fay, that " *this will involve the Church into the ut-* " *moft Confufion*, for want of Baptifm and

3

a Valid Ministry is the most pernicious Confusion, and infinitely greater than what can proceed from such Persons receiving valid Baptism and Holy Orders; and therfore, if the Premises are true the Risk must be run, for Truths of so great Importance must not be stifled, and made to give way to suppos'd Confusions; because, whatsoever mischief may arise, can never be the Result of Divine Truth (which is always Good and Beneficial) but of Mens Sins and Impieties, in usurping those Sacred Offices, which they never receiv'd any Commission to Act in. So that those who value the Order and Peace of the Church, ought not to disallow of the Invalidity of Lay Baptism, upon the Account of this Consequence, but rather to enquire seriously, whether Divine Revelation gives us any Foundation to believe, that such Baptisms are Good and valid; and if they are not, whether the Nulling of Holy Orders be a real Consequence therof; and if it be, they should assert and maintain it to the utmost of their power, nay even to Martyrdom it self, if the defending such a Truth did expose them to it, rather than suffer themselves to be destitute both of a *Christian Priesthood,* and *Christian Baptism.*

Obj. XI, BUT others say, that to a-void the fatal Consequences of adhering too rigorously to this Doctrine of Lay Baptisms being Invalid, the " *Authority of the* " *Powers Hierarchial are very Divine, and* " *the same which Christ had, not to the vio-* " *lation of his Laws, but to* **dispense** *with* " *them to* **Edification***, for which they may* " *be impower'd to Relax stated Rules, in cases* " *that appear necessary or expedient.* And that therfore, tho' *Heretical, Schismatical,* " *and Mimical Baptisms are done without,* " *nay, and against the consent of the* Hie-" *rarchy, and therfore are not intire, or* " *valid in themselves, yet they are made so* " *on the Post-Fact, by the Spiritual Powers,* " *so far, as that the External Rite shall not* " *be Reiterated; but as to any Spiritual* " *Graces they are not to be had thereby, till* " *those defective and Irregular Acts are sup-* " *ply'd, Righted and Confirmed, by the Chrism* " *of the Bishop, or Imposition of his Hands,* " *or such Rite by which he shall fix the Person* " *Baptiz'd into a State of Canonical Uni-* " *on with the Church.* So also, the Validity of Lay Baptism, " *as well to its Inter-* " *nal, as External Priviledges, stands on* " *the Authority of the Church's Power to* " *grant such License to Lay-men in Extre-* " *mities.* All which being consider'd, Lay-Baptisms

Baptifms ought now to be acknowledg'd Valid, efpecially to fuch as have been confirm'd by the Bifhop.

Anfw. THIS Objection is for the moft part in the very Words of a Learned and Reverend Oppofer, of One of the moft Poyfonous Books that, it may be, was ever fuffer'd to be Publifh'd in the Chriftian World, *falfly Intitul'd*, the **Rights of the Chriftian Church afferted** The worthy Author, who has done the Church good Service, in anfwering that pernicious Book, I dare fay, never defigned, that any thing in his moft Excellent Book fhould be conftru'd to favour our Lay-Baptifms, which are evidently *in oppofition* to the Divine Right of Epifcopacy, and for which our Hierarchial Powers have provided **no Act of Confirmation** So that in thefe Nations, Our Lay Baptizers and their Profelytes, can reap no benefit by any thing afferted in this Objection

I HAVE already, under the Corollary of the Third Propofition, declar'd my Reafons againft the difpenfing Power pleaded in this Objection; to which I fhall further add, That I acknowledge *the Divine Powers of the Hierarchy*, but with this Reftriction, that fince the fetling of the Canon of the Holy Scriptures, they are

for

for ever limited **in Things fundamental**
to that Rule, from which they have no Authority to Deviate, and consequently not to
dispense with any of the Essentials of Baptism, which without all doubt is a Fundamental of Christianity, such a *Dispensa-*
tion must be a *Violation* of Christ's Law,
and how that should be to *Edification* is
inconceiveable, since Christ our Great Law-
Giver, has provided Fundamentals sufficient for the Edification of his Church
in all circumstances whatsoever ; and obedience to his Laws about Fundamentals, is
most certainly the best Edification ; otherwise, He who is Omniscient, Wisdom it
self, would never have made such Laws :
and therfore with submission, ther seems
to be no necessity for impowering the
Governours of the Church *to " Relax his*
" stated Rules, no not in Cases that appear
" necessary or expedient. Besides, if Christ
has made stated Rules for the Essentials of
Christian Sacraments, without providing
for such pretended Cases of Necessity, the
Hierarchial Powers must certainly run a
great hazard of Sin, in attempting to
dispense with things, for which he has
made no Provision ; and the Persons
dispens'd with can have *no just satisfaction*
in such Dispensations, especially when the

seeming

seeming cause of them is removed, as it certainly is in the case of Persons baptiz'd by Laymen, contrary to the stated Rule who may afterwards obtain Episcopal Baptism agreeable to the Law of Christ, *if the Hierarchial Powers will but give them leave.*

THIS I say in opposition to those who affirm, that the Hierarchial Powers **are actually endowed** *with Authority to " dispense with Christ's Laws, and to Relax " stated Rules, in cases that appear necessary & " expedient* , which the Learned Author, whose Words they use, does not say. All that he intimates is only, that they **may be** impower'd to do so , which plainly shews, that he would not venture to affirm that they really are , and 'tis reasonable to believe, that upon second Thoughts he will not allow so much, as that they *may be* so impower'd , because what *may be, may not be,* as far as we know : nay, 'tis more agreeable to reveal'd Religion to say, that they are not so impower'd ; because, a thing of so great moment would never have been left out of the Divine Oracles, to be handed down to us thro' all Ages, by the **uncertain method** of Tradition only ; and therfore, 'tis very unsafe for us to trust in such [*may be's*] when the Re-

L 4 cei ing,

ceiving, or not Receiving, of *Spiritual Supernatural Priviledges and Benefits,* depends upon the Truth or Falfity of fuch a difpenfing Power, as it certainly does in the Adminiftration of Chriftian Sacraments. " *Heretical, Schifmatical and Mimical Bap-* " *tifms,* are in this Objection acknowledg'd to be " *not Entire or Valid in themfelves,* therfore in themfelves they are utterly and entirely Invalid (*by the Corollary* of the 3d Propofition.) It is alfo agreed, that " *as to* " *any Spiritual Graces they are not to be had, thereby till* &c. which is a plain Indication, that of **themfelves** they are of *no Efficacy* to the Purpofes of Chriftian Baptifm, the Adminiftration whereof is certainly efficacious for the conveyance of Spiritual Graces. Again, they are call'd here " *Defective* " *and Irregular Acts.* But why are they *Defective,* except but for their being uncapable of producing the proper Effects of true Baptifm? And why fhould they be term'd *Irregular Acts,* except only but for being contrary to the ftated Rule (or which is the fame) the Firft Inftitution of Chriftian Baptifm?

SO that the *External Rite* perform'd by thefe *Heretical, Schifmatical and Mimical Baptizers,* being thus acknowledg'd to be contrary to the Inftitution of Baptifm, and

utterly

utterly uncapable in it felf, of being the means to convey any *Spiritual Graces* what has it to do with Chriftian Baptifm? certainly it muft be a mere Nullity, and all one as if it had never been perform'd, becaufe, if it had no virtue to confer Spiritual Graces, it had no virtue to confer any *Benefit* at all; for, even the outward Priviledges are no Priviledges, when feparate from the Spiritual Graces. Thus, all Perfons, on whom the faid *External Rite* was perform'd, can receive by means therof, none of the Benefits of Chriftian Baptifm, which are all Spiritual and Supernatural, and confequently muft remain in the State of the Unbaptiz'd, till they receive true Chriftian Baptifm; which how they can receive without repeating the External Rite by a proper Adminiftrator, is utterly inconceivable. It is faid indeed, that " *thofe Defective and Irregular Acts,* (i. e. the External Rites of thofe Heretical, Schifmatical and Mimical Baptifms) *are Sup-* " *ply'd, Righted, and Confirm'd, by the Chrifm* " *of the Bifhop, or Impofition of his Hands,* " &c. For anfwer to which, I refer the Reader to *the Corollary of the 3d Propofition*; & further add, that this is only faid and not prov'd; and I believe never will, till it can be demonftrated that, that which before

was

was *no Baptism at all* in the Christian sense of the Word, is now made true Christian Baptism (without the Act of Baptization) merely by the Bishop's Chrism, or Imposition of his Hands. Either the first External Rite was the **One Baptism** the Scripture speaks of, or it was not; if it was, then it was Entire and Valid Baptism, and consequently wants no such Act of the Bishop to *supply and right it* ; but if it was not that **One Baptism**, then nothing can make it so, but the very Act of Baptization by a Christian Minister : for it may with *as much reason* be affirm'd, that Baptism is Administer'd really and truly by such Acts of the Bishop, to *all other Unbaptiz'd Persons* as well as to those ; and so at last, Baptism it self will be render'd needless, when the want of it can be *so easily supply'd* : but no less than a Divine Revelation will suffice to convince us, that this is true, and till that is produc'd we must continue to believe, that not all the Acts of the highest created Powers on Earth, are sufficient to make that which before was no Baptism, to become Christian Baptism, without the Act of Baptization by a proper Minister, as Christ has appointed in the Institution : And that consequently, those who never Receiv'd any other than

Lay

Lay Baptifm are ftill Unbaptiz'd, notwithftanding their being fuppos'd to have been
confirm'd by the Bifhop. As for the *Validity of Lay Baptifm,* that it " *ftands on*
" *the Authority of the Church's Power, to*
" *grant fuch Licenfe to Lay-men in Extre-*
" *mities* ; when it can be prov'd, that
*Chrift has Vefted his Church with fuch a
Power,* it will neceffarily follow, that Lay
Baptifm, *in Cafes of Extremity,* muft be
Valid upon that Foundation ; but even
then, *our Ordinary Lay Baptifms* muft be
Null and Void, becaufe they are deftitute
of the Plea *of Neceffity* in a Country where
Chriftian Priefts are to be had ; and therfore, 'tis in vain to claim any Benefit from
the fuppos'd Power of the Church, becaufe fhe her felf has not Authority to ex-
ercife this Power, except in 𝕰𝖝𝖙𝖗𝖊𝖒𝖎𝖙𝖎𝖊𝖘,
which God be prais'd we do not *yet* labour
under. But after all, 'tis dangerous to allow, that *this Power* was ever given to the
Church for Cafes of Extremity, becaufe,
fuch a Power would be an Occafion of de-
ftroying the very Unity of the Church,
and expofe her to the endlefs Divifions,
and Separations, which Hereticks and
Schifmaticks would make from her : for,
if by virtue of this fuppos'd Power, fhe
fhould once make a Canon to Licenfe Lay-
men

men to Adminifter Valid Baptifm in Cafes of Extremity, then fuch dividing Hereticks and Schifmaticks, calling their pretended *Scruples*, and *Tendernefſes of Con-
fcience*, by the Name of **Cafes of extremity**, would eftablifh the Validity of their
Lay Adminiftrations, upon the Authority
of the Church from whom they feparate,
and vindicate their Oppofitions to her, by
the Power which fhe in fuch cafe would
implicitly give to them. And fo every
private Perfon, after having blinded his
Underftanding by hearkening to Falfe
Teachers, might plead, that he was under
a **Necefſity** to feparate from the Church,
by reafon that he cannot overcome his
Scruples about her Doctrine and Worfhip;
And therfore might join himfelf to any
Congregation he fhould like beft, without the leaft fear of dividing from the
Church, becaufe, *where true Sacraments and
the Word of God are, there muft be a
true Church* ; and he could find proper
Sacraments Adminifter'd in thefe New
Congregations even by Lay Adminiftrators,
who Act by *the Authority of the Church
her felf.* This is to build the Church and
its Unity upon fo precarious a Foundation,
that we fhall never know what Schifm and
caufelefs Separation mean, tho' the Scripture
tells

tells us *ther are and will be such Sins*, and the Apostles pronouncing Damnation upon those who are guilty of such Sins (*Gal.* 5 20, 21.) will have no force and efficacy upon Men's Consciences, when they can once perswade themselves (as they too often do) that they separate *for Necessity*, and can *upon that very Account* receive Valid Sacraments from Lay Hands ; and then 'twill be in vain to say, that such Lay Administrations must be confirm'd by the Bishop before they can be Valid Sacraments, for it will be demanded, by what Authority the Bishop requires such Administrations to be confirm'd by him? and if good Testimonials from Holy Scripture are not produc'd for this purpose, the Bishop's *Supplying* and *Righting* such Irregular Acts will be made a Jest of, and the *Separatists* will conclude themselves as much in the Church as the Bishop himself, while they Administer and Receive as good Sacraments as he, since he cannot prove their Lay Administrations *necessary* to be *Confirm'd, Righted* and *Supply'd*, by imposition of his Hands, *&c.* On the contrary, if it had but been constantly asserted and defended, *That the Sacraments of the Christian Church are by Institution of such a Nature, that the Christian Priesthood is one Inseparable and*

Essential

Essential part of them, or, that the Divine Authority of the Administrator, is **as much** *and as durable a part of their Institution, as the very matter, or outward Elements of them.* If Men had been always taught, that *in the Sacraments, the Priest is* **as much** *the Representative of God the Giver, as the outward Elements are of the Graces given, and that consequently, these latter are no Christian Sacraments when separate from God's Authoriz'd Representative the Priest: And that the Church her self cannot by any Authority given to her, alter the nature of these things.* If these Topicks had been constantly insisted on, without *Triming* to please any Party of *Hereticks* or *Schismaticks* whatsoever, 'Tis more than probable, that Men would have been much more tender of the Unity of the Church, and more cautious of separating from her, than now we find they are; since how far soever their vain Curiosity might have prompted them to have follow'd *New fangled Lay Teachers* to please their itching Ears, yet the consideration of their being *destitute* of 𝕮𝖍𝖗𝖎𝖘𝖙𝖎𝖆𝖓 𝕾𝖆𝖈𝖗𝖆𝖒𝖊𝖓𝖙𝖘, might have terrify'd them from *withdrawing* from the Communion of the Christian Priesthood, and therby have prevented, at least, many of those *final Separations* from *the only salutary*

Communion,

Communion, which abundance of poor Wretches have fallen into, meerly thro' the falſe notion of better Edification, and vain belief of being ſure to find true Chriſtian Sacraments in communion with *their New ſet up Lay Teachers.* And 'tis juſtly to be fear'd, that the continual ſeparations from the Church in all Ages, and particularly in ours, have chiefly ſprung from this wretched Opinion of the meer *Opus Operatum* of Sacraments being real Sacraments, whether Adminiſter'd by a Prieſt or a Lay Man ; as if Chriſt's appointing the Order of Prieſthood in the Chriſtian Church, ſignify'd nothing at all, notwithſtanding 'twas the reſult of the moſt conſummate Wiſdom of our Great Law-giver.

BUT, becauſe 'tis pleaded from Scripture Inſtances, that Caſes of Neceſſity and Extremity, have taken place of Divine Inſtitutions, and that therfore Baptiſm, in Caſes of extream Neceſſity, may be Validly Adminiſter'd by a Lay-man, notwithſtanding the Inſtitution requires it to be Adminiſter'd by a Prieſt : and foraſmuch, as many Lay-baptiz'd Perſons encourage themſelves by ſuppoſing theirs to be a Caſe of Neceſſity, and conſequently that they have receiv'd true Chriſtian Baptiſm, tifm, I fhall therfore, in anfwer to the next Objection fhew, that thofe Inftances produc'd from Scripture are not parallel to Chriftian Baptifm, and that ther is nothing in them that can favour Lay Baptifm, even in Cafes of greateft Extremity.

Obj XII. IN the Inftitution of the Paffover, it was appointed that the Jews fhould eat the Pafchal Lamb *"with their Loins " girded, their Shoes on their Feet, and their " Staff in their Hand,*Exod. 12. 11. which fignifies a ftanding Pofture : The Church of the Jews afterwards chang'd this Pofture into that of Leaning or Lying along ; and our Saviour finding this Cuftom prevail'd in his Days, comply'd with it when he celebrated the Paffover, *(Mat.* 26. 20.) Which plainly fhews, that we may many times comply with the Churches changing even a Divine Inftitution for a Human one ; and why not therfore with the Churches allowing of Lay-Baptifm in Cafes of Neceffity ? Again, our Saviour reproving the Jews for their over Rigid Nicenefs in obferving the Divine Inftitution of the Sabbath, tells them, *That David " when he had need did take and Eat the " Shew Bread, and gave to them that were " with him which was not lawful for him " to eat, neither for them that were with him,*

" but

" *but for the Priests alone* (St. *Mat.* 12. 4. St. *Mark* 2. 25, 26.) making *David's* Neceſſity a ſufficient Reaſon, for diſpenſing at that time with God's own Poſitive Inſtitution about the Shew-Bread. And further, our Bleſſed Lord upon the ſame occaſion reproving the *Jews*, ſays, that *God will have Mercy and not Sacrifice*, (St. *Mat.* 12. 7.) Which is ſufficient to inſtruct us, that in Caſes of Neceſſity, the Poſitive Inſtitutions of God himſelf muſt be ſometimes diſpens'd with, for the ſupply of our wants, and conſequently, that Baptiſm in caſes of Neceſſity, where a Prieſt cannot be had, may be Validly Adminiſter'd by a Lay-man, to ſupply the Spiritual Wants of thoſe who are Unbaptiz'd.

Anſw. THIS Objection conſiſts of ſo many particulars, that 'twill be neceſſary for me to conſider it, in the ſame order wherein it lyes. And,

1ſt. THE Poſture of ſtanding to Eat the Paſchal Lamb was no more than a *Temporary* Inſtitution, peculiar to the Celebration of the Firſt Paſſover in *Egypt*, the very Night the *Jews* were to Depart out of that Country. This is plain, from the reaſon of God's appointing them to Eat it in ſuch a Poſture of Travellers, *in haſte, viz.* becauſe he would " *paſs through*

M " *the*

' the Land of *Egypt* that *Night*, and *Smite*
' all the *First-born* in *Egypt* both of *Man*
" and *Beast*, (ver. 12.) which would have
such an Effect upon the *Egyptians*, that
they would be very pressing and Urgent
upon the Children of *Israel* to depart out
of their Country to be rid of their Company, for whose sake they had suffered so
many and great Plagues, and were now
depriv'd of their First-born, throughout
all their Houses and Families, see *Exod.*
12. from *ver.* 29. to *ver.* 34. And, if the
Children of *Israel* had not been that Night
in such a Travelling Posture, they would
not have been prepar'd for so sudden and
hasty a departure, as the distracted and
terrify'd *Egyptians* oblig'd them to, wherby they might have been expos'd to abundance of Inconveniencies, both from the
fury of the *Egyptians*, and their own Un-
preparedness for a Midnight Journey: And
therfore, that they might not be thus in-
commoded, God requir'd them to eat the
Paschal Lamb " **in haste**, *with their Loins*
" *girded, their Shoes on their Feet, and their*
" *Staff in their Hand*, to be ready for their
Journey at any warning that should be
given them that Night; but after their
departure the Reason of this Appointment
ceas'd, and therfore so did the Appointment

ment it felf, and confequently was no longer binding and obliging : and we never find this Travelling Pofture repeated in any of the after Celebrations of the Paffover: but that it was only a *Temporary Inftitution,* peculiar to that Firft Celebration, I appeal to the Learned Jews both Ancient and Modern, and alfo to our beft Commentators upon the place, (fee Bifhop *Patrick, Grotius, Diodati, Pools Synopfis,*&c.) to whom I refer the Reader, that I may not be more Prolix upon this Subject.

THE Pofture of Standing then, being not enjoyn'd to be conftantly us'd, *was no Effential Part* of the Inftitution of the Paffover, and therfore 'twas afterwards *indifferent* what Pofture the Jews fhould Eat the Pafchal Lamb in ; for which reafon, their Church certainly had power to appoint any *innocent Pofture* fhe fhould think fit ; and fince *Leaning or Lying along* was determin'd by her, and prevail'd in our Saviour's Days, and he was pleas'd to conform to it, we ought to follow his Example in complying with fuch Inftitutions of the Church as are not *contrary* to the Law of God. But this Inftance do's not allow us to comply with the Church's changing a Divine Inftitution for a Human one ; becaufe, the Church of

the

the Jews did not herein **change** a *Divine* into a *Human Institution* ; for, the Posture of Standing was then *no Divine Appointment because not Essential to the Passover,* and therfore the Church of the Jews did not **change** this into another Ceremony, but **appoint** the *indifferent Ceremony* of Lying or Leaning, when ther was *no Divine Institution* at that time, obliging them to any other Posture.

AND therfore, we ought not, *from the Authority of this Instance,* to comply with the Church's allowing of Lay Baptism in Cases of Necessity, because Baptism by a **Priest** is Essential to Christian Baptism, and as much obliging as the Institution of **Water** it self, during the utmost term of the Christian Dispensation, as I have prov'd under the 1st and 2d Propositions. And a Lay-man's Baptizing to confer Supernatural Benefits, is **no indifferent Circumstance** in the Power of Man to determine and appoint, as was the Posture of Lying or Leaning along, when the Church of the Jews appointed it; and therfore, from that Church's Example and our Saviour's conformity thereto, no Argument can be drawn to support the Validity of Lay Baptism, even in Cases of greatest Necessity, because the quality of the Person who

is

is Authoriz'd to Baptize for Supernatural Purposes, is determin'd by no other than a mere Positive Divine Institution. And no Case of Necessity whatsoever can determine any other means for the conveyance *of Supernatural Benefits,* than what are already reveal'd to us, except God shall be pleas'd to make some New Revelation of his Will for such a Purpose.

2. A S for the Instance of *David* and his Mens Eating the Shew-Bread; least Men should from hence encourage themselves to break through all the Divine Laws to supply their Necessities, 'tis necessary to consider, what Circumstances of Necessity will excuse our breaking a mere Positive Institution of Religion.

First, THEN, considering that all God's Positive Institutions are appointed for our Obedience, nothing can excuse us from the Breach of any one of them, but some other **more incumbent** Duty, which at the same time stands in competition with the Positive Duty.

Secondly, THE means of supplying our Necessities, must either be such as are of a *natural Efficiency,* or else efficacious by virtue of a *Divine Institution,* Administer'd just as God himself has apppointed.

BOTH these circumstances concurr'd

M 3   in

in *David* and his Mens eating the Shew-Bread, and not one of them is to be found in Lay Baptism. For,

1*st*. T H O' by the Positive Law, 'twas not lawful for any but the Priests to eat it, yet by the Law of Nature and Reveal'd Religion too, it was necessary to feed the necessitous Hungry ; and *David* and his Men, wanting Bread, and ther being at that time no other to supply their Necessity (1 *Sam.* 21. 6) the Priest gave him the Hallow'd Bread, that so the Law of Charity to the Lives of Men, enforc'd by a double Obligation, *viz.* by the Law of Nature and of Reveal'd Religion, might take place of the *mere Positive Law* about the Shew Bread, which had no other Obligation than from the Positive Institution only, with which the said Law of Charity stood at that time in competition ; and this is exactly agreeable to what the Learn'd Dr. *Hammond* says, in his Paraphrase upon St. *Mat.* 12. 3, 4 which because so very apposite to this purpose, I shall here transcribe for the Readers Information. His Words are these, " *Remem-* " *ber the Story of David,* 1 *Sam.* 21. 6. " *and by that you will discern that the Case* " *of Hunger was Excepted, and Reserv'd in* " *the Law concerning Holy Days or Things* ; " *For*

" *For there David and his Company being*
" *press'd with Hunger, were by the Priest*
" *allow'd to Eat the Shew Bread, which*
" *being consecrated did particularly belong to*
" *the Priest,* Levit. 24. 9. *yet might it*
" *seems (by the intention of the Law-giver)*
" *be by him imploy'd in any charitable use, for*
" *the Relief of others, as long as there were*
" *more ready consecrated for the Sacred Uses,*
" 1 Sam. 21. 5. *And accordingly, tho' the*
" *Priest pretended not to dispense with any*
" *(so much as Ritual) Part of God's Law*
" *(as appears by the exception interpos'd by*
" *him* ver. 4. *If the Young Men have kept*
" *themselves from Women) yet he doubts not*
" *to give them freely of the Consecrated*
" *Bread ; thereby assuring us, that it was*
" *as Lawful for the Priest to give some part*
" *of the Consecrated Bread to relieve the*
" *Hungry, as to Eat it himself; and so that*
" *in the Law of Holy Things, not being*
" *touch'd by any but the Priests, the Case of*
" *Hunger or Distress was reserv'd, in which*
" *it might by the Priest be lawfully given to*
" *others.* Thus far that learn'd Author.
But nothing of all this occurs in Lay
Baptism : for the Positive Law requires
that Baptism should be Administer'd by
a Priest of God's Appointment ; and
ther is no Law of but equal, much less

of

of *greater* Obligation that requires a Layman to Baptize at all : Natural Religion does not oblige him to Baptize, becaufe Baptifm is no part of Natural Religion ; and as for Reveal'd Religion, that has not requir'd him to Baptize; and therfore in Cafes of greateft Neceffity, if he does Baptize, he acts *without any Duty incumbent on him*, contrary to a Pofitive Inftitution, which is no Ways confiftent with this Inftance of *David* and his Men.

2*dly*, THE means of fupplying the Neceffity of *David* and his Men was Bread, which has a Natural Phyfical Efficiency to fatisfie Hunger, and confequently to preferve Humane Life ; but Baptifm has no Natural Phyfical Power to convey to us the *Forgivenefs of Sins*, and *the Gift of the Holy Ghoft* : its Efficacy for fuch Supernatural Purpofes depends only on a Pofitive Inftitution, and therfore, *is not at all parallel* to the Inftance of the Shew-Bread ; and confequently, under this Second Rule, nothing can be inferr'd from *David* and his Mens Eating that Bread to a Lay man's Adminiftring Valid Baptifm, becaufe they are things of quite different Natures and Effects; and no ways applicable to one another. So that to bring Lay-Baptifm to this Second Rule, it muft be prov'd Efficacious

cious *by virtue of a Divine Inſtitution Adminiſter'd juſt as God himſelf has appointed :*
but this can never be done, becauſe ther
is *no Divine Inſtitution of Lay Baptiſm.*

IN ſhort, to ſum up all that I have
ſaid or need to ſay about this Inſtance of the
Shew Bread : Bread, before 'twas ſet apart
for Sacred Uſes, was common for all Men
to Eat for the ſatisfying of their Hunger ;
but the Adminiſtration of Baptiſm for
Supernatural Purpoſes was never thus common : the Prieſts giving the Shew-Bread,
when *no other was to be had,* was then
an Act of Charity, to which he was
oblig'd by the very Law of Nature, enforc'd by the Reveal'd Will of God, But
Lay Baptiſm is no Duty incumbent on us
either by the Law of Nature or Reveal'd
Religion ; the Law of Nature dictates
nothing to us about Baptiſm for Supernatural Purpoſes, and Reveal'd Religion is
wholly ſilent about *Lay Baptiſm for ſuch
Ends.* The Shew Bread had a Phyſical
Natural Efficiency to ſatisfie Hunger and
preſerve Life, and therfore the Prieſt had
encouragement to give it, becauſe he had
no reaſon to doubt of its good Effect ;
but *Baptiſm* has no Natural Phyſical Efficiency for Supernatural and Spiritual Graces, its Effects are purely owing to a
Poſitive

Positive Institution only, and therfore we have no encouragement to hope for its Effects, when the Institution is not observ'd in all its Essential Parts, as it certainly is not when a Layman Administers. Further, in the Eating of the Shew-Bread ther was *no contradiction* ; the Priest did not give it to be eaten contrary to the Positive Institution, with a design by so doing to observe the same Positive Institution; but in Lay Baptism ther's a perfect Contradiction; The Positive Institution of Baptism is broken, that by so doing the same Positive Institution may be observ'd and kept whole. From all which 'tis very clear and evident, that the Eating of the Shew-Bread, and the Administration of Valid Baptism (in Cases of Necessity) by a Lay-hand, are things infinitely different in their Nature, and consequently not at all applicable the one to the other. To which I beg leave to add, that the Eating of the Shew-Bread, was no *Authoritative Administration for the conveyance of Supernatural Grace*, as Valid Baptism most certainly is : And therfore 'tis no wonder, that God put a good Construction upon *David* and his Mehs Eating that Bread to satisfie their hunger, when no other was to be had ; and yet upon all occasions, severely punish'd the *Sacrilegious Usurpations* of every one that

that attempted to officiate in such Authoritative Administrations, as he had appointed for the conveyance of Spiritual Benefits; the *great Necessities* that urg'd them thus to officiate, were never admitted or allowed of, so much as but to mitigate their Crime, much less to make their Administrations Valid : This is apparently evident in the Case of *Saul*'s taking upon him to *offer a Sacrifice* in his great Distress, when his Enemies were coming upon him, when he might have been slain before he could make his peace with God, when the Priest *Samuel* was not present; when he had waited and strove so long, that he at last forc'd himself to offer a Sacrifice to procure the Divine Favour. We see, that all this 𝔑𝔢𝔠𝔢𝔰𝔰𝔦𝔱𝔶 and the 𝔞𝔟𝔰𝔢𝔫𝔠𝔢 𝔬𝔣 𝔱𝔥𝔢 𝔓𝔯𝔦𝔢𝔰𝔱 ! this eager desire to obtain a Blessing ! was no excuse for his assuming the Priest's Office; God would and did punish him for it, by rending the Kingdom from him, and giving it to another as you may see in 1 *Sam.* 13. This is a standing Example, upon which we should always fix our Eyes, and therby learn, that however God may excuse in some cases of Necessity, he will never do it in such great Instances, as the taking upon our selves to Administer, or willingly concurring with those who do Minister in the Priest's Office, without being *called of God, as was* Aaron.

3. As

3. A S for that other Text, where 'tis
said *I will have Mercy and not Sacrifice*, it
will as little serve for the Validity of Lay
Baptism as the rest. For the occasion of
our Saviour's using those Words, and the
place of Scripture from whence he quoted
them, do evidently prove, that the Design
of this Text is only to convince us, *that
such Positive Institutions as are here call'd by
the Name of* 𝔖𝔞𝔠𝔯𝔦𝔣𝔦𝔠𝔢, *were never appointed to frustrate and make void our Obligation
to the Genuine Moral Duties of Natural Religion, particularly those of Justice and E-
quity, and of compassion and charity to the
Necessities and Wants of our Fellow Crea-
tures ; but that on the contrary, our Want
of such Excellent Moral Virtues, and our
being of an unjust, uncharitable and cruel
temper, will make those Positive Duties when
perform'd by us, both loathsome and abominable in the sight of God.*

T H I S I say is evident, First from the
occasion of our Saviour's referring the Jews
to that Text, " *I will have Mercy and not
Sacrifice* ; for the Disciples being hungry
plucked the Ears of Corn on the Sabbath-
Day, which the Pharisees observing, affirm-
ed, that it was a Breach of the Sabbath,
and therfore unlawful for them to do at
that time ; but our Saviour (who very
well knew the barbarous Cruelty of their
temper)

temper*)* bid them remember the Cafe of *David* and his Mens Eating the Shew-Bread, *&c.* and then tells them, " *if ye had* " *known what this meaneth,* " *I will have* " *Mercy and not Sacrifice, ye would not have* " *condemned the* 𝕲𝖚𝖎𝖑𝖙𝖑𝖊𝖘𝖘, St. *Mat.* 1 2. 7. Whereby he prov'd the Innocence of his Difciples, that they had not at all broken the Sabbath, by thus plucking the Ears of Corn to affwage their hunger; and that confequently, the *Moral Duties* of Mercy, and Works of abfolute Neceffity, were never intended by the Pofitive Inftitution of the Sabbath, to be reckon'd as Breaches of the Duty of Reft, which God requir'd on that Holy Day.

2dly. THE Place of Scripture from whence our Lord quoted thofe Words is *Hofea* 6. 6. *I defired Mercy and not Sacrifice,* This does not mean that God did not require Sacrifice; for 'tis plain that he did require it, and all other Pofitive Duties fignified by that general Word; and the Jews at that very time were bound to obferve and obey all the Pofitive Inftitutions of the Mofaic Law, under no lefs penalty than that of " *Curfed be he that confirmeth not* " *all the Words of this Law to do them.* Deut. 27. 26. So that the *not Sacrifice* here muft
mean

mean [**not only Sacrifice**] or [**not Sa-crifice alone**] and therfore , the plain Paraphrate of this Text is " *I defired or Re-* " *quir'd* **not only Sacrifice**, *not only your* " *Obedience to my mere Pofitive Inftitutions,* " *but alfo your Obfervance of my Moral Law of* " *Mercy and Kindnefs.* 'Twas the want of this and other Moral Virtues, together with their being guilty of cruel Murders, Robberies, and other Immoralities, that God complain'd of, almoft throughout this whole Chapter, and for which he abhor'd their very Sacrifices, tho' they were of his own appointment, and they were then bound and oblig'd to offer them to him : This is alfo confirm'd by *Micah* 6. & *Ifa.* I. 11, 12, 13, 14, 15, &c. All which being duly confider'd, fufficiently declares, the fence and meaning of [*I will have Mercy and not Sacrifice.*] that the defign therof is not to make void our Obligation to obey the Divine Pofitive Inftitutions ; but to convince us, that the *Moral Duties of Natural Religion*, reinforc'd by Divine Revelation, are fo far from being incon-fiftent with, That they muft conftantly accompany and attend our Obedience to fuch Pofitive Inftitutions, and that our Approaches to God in his Pofitive Inftitu-tions, without fuch Moral Virtues, are

fo

ſo far from being accepted that they are hated and abhorr'd by him.

AND therfore, all that (at moſt) can be inferr'd from thoſe Words of our Saviour is, that *when a mere Poſitive Inſtitution ſtands in neceſſary competition with a Moral Duty of natural Religion, reinforc'd by Divine Revelation, then the mere Poſitive Inſtitution muſt give way to the Moral Duty for that time and circumſtance.*

NOW then to *try to* apply this to the Caſe before us. Ther's a Divine Poſitive Inſtitution, requiring Baptiſm to be Adminiſter'd by One who has Chriſt's Commiſſion for ſo doing. This Baptiſm is appointed to be a Means of confering ſuch merciful Graces and Benefits, as our miſerable Nature, could never have made any claim or title to, and which all the powers of Nature could never have beſtow'd on us. It happens, that a Perſon wanting theſe ineſtimable benefits moſt earneſtly deſires to obtain them by Baptiſm ; but a Miniſter with Chriſt's Commiſſion, is neither now, nor likely hereafter to be had: what then muſt be done in this extream Neceſſity ? Why ſays the Objector, *God will have Mercy and not Sacrifice :* and therfore, ſince Sacrifice now ſtands in competition

with

with Mercy, the Sacrifice muſt give way to Mercy; the Divine Authority of the Adminiſtrator muſt not now be inſiſted on; but the Mercies and Favours muſt be beſtowed on the Perſon by a Lay man's Adminiſtring Baptiſm to him. This ſeems to be well ſaid; but upon examination 'twill be found, that no ſuch thing can be juſtly inferr'd from this Text, becauſe, the *Mercy* there ſpoken of, is a *Moral Duty* of Natural Religion, and to be extended to the Indigent and Neceſſitous by *Natural means*; but the *Mercies* to be receiv'd by Chriſtian Baptiſm, are infinitely above all *Natural Religion*, and conſequently not to be convey'd by any *Natural means.* The reaſon why we are oblig'd to perform thoſe Natural Acts of Mercy, even when they ſeem to run counter to ſome mere Poſitive Inſtitution, is becauſe *Natural Conſcience* dictates this Duty, and *Divine Revelation* has reinforc'd its Obligation; whereas we are bound to obſerve a *Poſitive Inſtitution* merely upon the account of a Divine Law promulg'd to us, without which we could never have been oblig'd to the Obſervation of it. But this Reaſon is wholly wanting in Lay Baptiſm; For *Natural Conſcience* dictates nothing to us about beſtowing of *Supernatural Mercies,*

by

by means of any kind of Baptiſm whatſoever; and as for Reveal'd Religion, that
is wholly ſilent about a Lay-man's being
ever capable of conveying ſuch Mercies
to us by means of Baptiſm ; ſo that the
Lay-man has this Duty incumbent on him
neither by the Law of Nature, nor of Divine Revelation ; and therfore, if he baptizes for Spiritual Purpoſes, *that he may
ſhew mercy,* he ventures to do otherwiſe
than the Poſitive Inſtitution of Baptiſm requires, and at the ſame time is deſtitute
of any the leaſt encouragement from the
Text objeƈted, becauſe ther is no Law
either Natural or Reveal'd that obliges
him ſo to do.

BUT further, when God will *have
Mercy and not Sacrifice* ; it is not intended, that one or more Eſſential Parts of a
mere Poſitive Inſtitution, ſhould be more
neceſſary and obliging to us than the other
Eſſential Parts therof. No, all that God
then requires of us is, to prefer a Moral
before a mere poſitive Duty, as is evident
from what I have already ſaid on this Sub-
jeƈt. But our Aſſertors of the Validity
of Lay Baptiſm in Caſes of Neceſſity, do
unavoidably run themſelves into this In-
conſiſtency, of making one or more Eſſential Parts of a mere Poſitive Inſtitution,

N   to

to be of *greater Neceſſity* and Obligation than another Eſſential Part of the ſame Inſtitution ; for, they make *Water* and *the Form of Baptiſm* to be more neceſſary and obliging, than the *Divine Authority* of *the Adminiſtrator* : but this Notion I have already endeavoured to confute in the *Second Propoſition*; to which I refer the Reader, and deſire him here to obſerve, how very diſagreeable this is with God's requiring *Mercy*, a Moral Duty, *and not Sacrifice*, a mere Poſitive One : For 'tis in effect to make God ſay, inſtead of [*I will have Mercy and not Sacrifice,*] *I will have Sacrifice, and not Sacrifice* ; ſince ther is not one of thoſe Eſſential Parts of Baptiſm but what is merely of Poſitive Inſtitution. This, of making one Eſſential Part of ſuch an Inſtitution, to give way to the other Eſſential Parts therof in Caſes of neceſſity, without a particular Revelation of God's Will for ſo doing, is ſo ſtrange, ſo unſcriptural a Practice, that ther is not One Example of it in all the Sacred Writings of the Old and New Teſtament, from the firſt Chapter of *Geneſis* to the laſt of the *Revelations*; but on the contrary, we have a flagrant inſtance of God's puniſhing this Practice in the Perſon of *Saul*, who in his 𝕹𝖊𝖈𝖊𝖘𝖘𝖎𝖙𝖞 that he might obtain 𝕸𝖊𝖗𝖈𝖞,

made

made one Eſſential part of a poſitive Inſtitution, to give way to another of its
Eſſential Parts ; for the Prieſt, one Eſſential
Part of the poſitive Inſtitution of Burnt-
Offerings, being abſent, he reckon'd the
Burnt-Offering to be more Eſſential than
the Adminiſtration of the Prieſt, and
therfore *offered a Burnt-Offering himſelf* ;
for which raſh Action *Samuel* ſaid to him,
Thou haſt done fooliſhly, (i. e. wickedly) *thou
haſt not kept* (but haſt broken) *the Commandment of the Lord thy God,* &c. ——
Thy Kingdom ſhall not continue, &c. 1 *Sam.*
13. 11, 12, 13, 14. Here his endeavour
to obtain Mercy, by means of *but part of
a mere poſitive Duty,* is, notwithſtanding
the urgency of his neceſſitous Circumſtances, branded with the Name of a fooliſh
wicked Action ; and becauſe 'twas not
attended with the other Eſſential Part, *viz.
the Miniſtration of the Prieſt,* was ſo far
from being eſteem'd a Valid Offering to
God, that it prov'd inſtead of a means of
Mercy, a Judgment and a Curſe to the
Offerer and his Poſterity.

THUS we ſee, that tho' God will have
us ſometimes extend *our Mercy* rather than
offer *Sacrifice :* yet when **Mercy** is to be obtain'd **from him** *by means of Sacrifice,* i. e.
ſuch mere poſitive Duties as he has requir'd,

he

he will not grant us the Mercy we sue for, by means of *but part of such Sacrifice* ; no' we must either beg it of him by our Observance of *the whole Institution*, or else when we cannot have the whole, sit down contented till we can, since he has declar'd his abhorrence of such *partial Sacrifices*, and therby taught us that they are *no Sacrifices at all.* 'Tis worth while to observe here, what *Samuel* tells *Saul*, (after he had reprov'd him for breaking God's Commandment about Burnt-Offerings) *for now*, (says he) *would the Lord have established thy Kingdom upon* Israel *for ever*, 1 Sam. 13. 13. ——— As much as if he had said, " *If thou hadst*
" *not attempted to gain the Divine Favour*
" *by so unwarrantable an Action ; if thou*
" *hadst been patient in thy Necessity, and not*
" *endeavour'd to render God propitious to*
" *thee by such an unlawful Method ; He is a*
" *God of Mercy, and would not have imputed*
" *Sin to thee for want of a Burnt Offering,*
" *when it could not be had according to his*
" *Institution; but on the contrary, would have*
" *esteem'd thy not medling therin to be an*
" *Act of Obedience to his Command ; and*
" *consequently (tho' ther had been no Burnt*
" *Offering made to him) would have been*
" *gracious and merciful to thee and thy Chil-*
" *dren after thee ; and as a Reward of thy*
" *Faith*

" *Faith and Obedience, would have establish'd*
" *the Kingdom to thee and thy Sons for ever.*
This I say is plainly the scope and meaning
of *Samuel*'s Words to *Saul* ; wherby we
also are encourag'd not to distrust the
Divine Goodness, but constantly and pati-
ently to wait and pray for it, without presuming to endeavour to obtain it by *partial
Sacrifice*, when we are under such sad circumstances, as not to be able to seek for it by
whole Burnt Offerings; when we cannot have
entire Baptism according to the Institution ; when there is no Priest to Administer
it to us; then 'tis a greater Act of Faith
and Obedience, to refuse than to accept
of supposed Baptism from a Lay hand :
Nay, for one who knows the Nature and
Extent of the Institution of Christian Baptism, to accept of, or acquiesce in Lay Baptism in Cases of suppos'd Necessity, 'tis a
great presumption ; because, 'tis expecting
God's Mercy to be convey'd by such Hands,
as *he has not appointed* for that purpose,
and to whose Ministration he never requir'd
our obedience ; 'Tis the superstition of
making that absolutely necessary to salvation which God has not made so ; as if
when we want those means which he has
appointed, he could not extend his Favours
and Graces without them ; as if ther were

a *greater degree* of Holineſs in Water, and a Form of Words, than in the Inſtitution of the Chriſtian Prieſthood ; as if none could be ſaved without the former, but every body without the latter ; as if Water could be a means of Graces *given*, without the mediation of one who do's truly *perſonate* God the *Giver*. In ſhort, 'tis Superſtition, nay and Preſumption too, to expect Mercy by means of but **part** of a Sacrifice, when God appointed that the **whole** ſhould be the means of obtaining that Mercy. And 'tis ſo exactly parallel to *Saul*'s caſe, and ſo infinitely different from the deſign of the Text objected, that we may very fairly conclude, that Lay. Baptiſm cannot be Valid even in Caſes of Neceſſity; it cannot be ſufficient, " *to ſup-* " *ply the Spiritual Wants of thoſe who are* " *Unbaptiz'd*, becauſe ther's no compariſon between the *Natural Means* of Admini-ſtring to the ordinary wants of the Ne-ceſſitous and Indigent, and the *ſupernatural appointed means* of ſupplying the *Spiritual Wants* of the Unbaptiz'd; for theſe latter are of ſo extraordinary a Nature, that no leſs than Mercies Supernatural are ſuffici-ent for ſo great a purpoſe ; and therfore, no other method muſt be uſed to obtain ſuch Mercies, than what he who is to

beſtow

beſtow them has appointed. *Obedience* in this caſe *is better than Sacrifice, eſpecially* than ſuch a falſe Burnt-Offering, as *Saul,* in the inſtance above-mention'd, preſum'd to offer to God : and may we all take warning by his Puniſhment not to confine God to our Will worſhip, not to meddle in his Poſitive Inſtitutes, and expect that he ſhould concur with our fooliſh and preſumptuous interpoſing, in ſuch Miniſtrations as he has confin'd to the Authority and Adminiſtration of his, and his Chriſt's appointed Prieſts and Miniſters only.

I CONCLUDE this Appendix, Moſt earneſtly intreating the moſt Reverend, the Right Reverend, and Reverend, **Governours** and **Miniſters** of Chriſt over his Flock in all parts of the **Univerſal** Church, The **Prieſts** *of the moſt high God!* who are duly Authoriz'd to repreſent and make viſible to us, the once viſible, but now inviſible **Prieſthood** *of the great high Prieſt of our Profeſſion Chriſt Jeſus ! who have not taken this Honour unto themſelves without being call'd of God, as was Aaron !* who are therfore the delegated **Ambaſſadours** *for Chriſt,* and appointed **Stewards** *of the Myſteries* of God, to whom he has given the **Keys,**

and committed the Cuftody of the **Two great Seals** *of the Kingdom of Heaven, fo that whatfoever they fhall bind on Earth fhall be bound in Heaven, and whatfoever they fhall loofe on Earth fhall be loofed in Heaven!* I humbly befeech them, in the *Bowels of Jefus Chrift*, to confider the great Dignity of their High and Holy Calling, and their **unalienable** Right to Adminifter thofe **Sacraments**, which the infinite Wifdom of our great Law-giver has appropriated to their facred Function. For If the miniftration of the Sacraments is not **effential** to their Office, and **their Office effential** to the Miniftration of Valid Sacraments, what fignifies the Inftitution of the *Priefthood*, and to what purpofe did our Bleffed Lord promife to be with his Priefts and concur with their Miniftrations *to the End of the World?* If the prefumptuous Miniftrations of Laymen acting of themfelves, or in oppofition to the Church and her Priefts, is not inconfiftent with the Nature and Property of True Sacraments : or if they can be *True and Valid* Sacraments when given by their Hands, how, and by what means, fhall we be convinc'd, of the neceffity of the Chriftian Priefthood to the Church by Divine Inftitution, and its perpetuity till
the

the confummation of all things ? How
fhall we be perfwaded to value the Miniftrations of a Prieft more than thofe of a
Lay-man, and what Arguments can be
produc'd for the prefervation of the *Unity*
of the Church, and to keep us from eternal
Schifms and Separations from her ? Your
long filence in not afferting and defending
the *Dignity of your Office*, and the *unalienable* Nature of thofe Sacraments which
Chrift has infeparably annex'd therto, tho'
it may have proceeded from a Notion of
Humility and Modefty, *that you might not
be thought to preach up your felves; but Chrift
Jefus the Lord* ; Yet (with fubmiffion be
it fpoken) feems to have been the occafion of *much Ignorance* among the Laity of
the nature of Schifm, and their duty to
you, and confequently of encouraging the
Enemies of the Clergy and their great Ma-
fter in Heaven, to blafpheme him, and
trample the Authority you have from him
under their Feet. Atheifm, Deifm, Pro-
phanenefs, Blafphemy, and Sacrilege, are
now grown Impudent, and Barefac'd, Bold,
and Rampant ; they fcorn any longer to
dwell in Obfcurity and Darknefs, when
they are become the fafhionable accom-
plifhments of *our pretended great Wits* ! *and
Men of diftinguifhed Senfe and Judgment* !
They

They have a grand defign in hand, (and their Emiffaries have profecuted it but with too much fuccefs) to reprefent your Office every where and to all forts of Men, as Tyranny, Impofture, and Ufurpation; to wreft the Sacraments out of your Hands, that you may become ufelefs and infignificant ; to make the giddy Multitude believe that all you do is nothing but *Priefcraft*, to bring and keep them under a worfe than Egyptian Bondage ; to expofe you to the Rage and Fury of an *ungovernable Mob*, and fo at laft to hifs you, and all *rezeal'd Religion*, off of the Stage of this World. What elfe mean their feveral execrable Books and Pamphlets that are now induftrioufly publifh'd, of fet purpofe to decry your Office, and ridicule your Miniftrations? How fhall the Ignorant be defended from their Infection, but by the Antidote, which fome of you, both by Books and Sermons, have already begun to apply, couragioufly following the Example of the great St. *Paul*, who *magnified his Office*, and therby the Authority of Jefus Chrift who fent him? God be praifed for thefe happy beginnings, thefe firft noble performances in maintaining your Office & in defence of the *true Rights of the Chriftian Church*, depofited in your Hands by the

great

ject) *did grant, that such Baptisms are not wholly Valid, because, that Council Canon 38, requir'd Lay Baptiz'd Persons to be PER-FECTED by Imposition of the Bishops Hands* [*See Prelim.ⁿ Disc. Page 12.*] *Now this their Concession, whether 'twas the true sense of that Canon or no, I thought convenient to make use of as an Argument against them, to prove that Imposition of the Bishop's Hands, or Confirmation only, cannot possibly give entire Validity to that Lay Baptism which was partly Invalid before And this is no other than* Argumentum ad Hominem, *which I had never made use of; if it had not been pleaded from that Council, that I ought not to require Episcopal Baptism, because, the Bishop having confirm'd me, that Act of his gave entire Validity to the Lay Baptism administer'd to me in my Infancy, tho' it was partly Invalid, before such Act of Confirmation.*

————— Whereas PERFECTED *in the sense of the Council and those times, only signifies* Finished *and* Consummated, *as all Lawful Baptisms were thought to be by Chrism and Imposition of Hands, which in those Days was immediately perform'd after Baptism, or as soon after as possibly could be ——— Again in*

Page 108 & 109. *ther's another Passage which possibly may be cavil'd at, viz.* How a SINFUL Act should be VALID *for supernatural* "Purposes is utterly inconceivable, nay, 'tis abominable to affirm *it. For some will say this is inconclusive, 'tis no argument, because many sinful Acts are certainly Valid ; as the Marriage of Minors without, and against the consent of Parents ; a Priest's administring the Sacraments of Baptism and the Eucharist to adult Persons not duly qualified, and the like ; but the Answer to this is easie, for these sinful Acts, are not Sins against the very Essence of the Institutions of Marriage, &c. but only against some accidental circumstance, But the sinful Act I am speaking of in the forecited passage, is a Sin against the very Essence of the* Positive Institution of Christian Baptism, *and therfore not parallel with those Instances.*

3dly *and Lastly, in the Appendix.*

Page 135. *and forward in answer to the* 10th Objection, *I have attempted to Prove the Validity of Holy Orders conferr'd on Unbaptiz'd Persons. What I have propos'd in order thereto, I desire the judicious Lovers of Truth to interpret only as an Essay ; I am not so fond of any thing I have said about it, as to strive with those who differ from me, nay more, if it should be generally condemn'd by Learned Men I shall acquiesce, acknowledging that they argue well who say, that 'tis suppos'd a Man ought to be a Member, before he can be a Minister of Christ in his Church.*

What I have said in the following and other Parts of this Book, in general Terms, against the Churches Power, to give Authority to a Layman for the Administration of Valid Baptism in Cases of extream Ne-

cessity,

To the READER.

cessity, *I think necessary by way of precaution here to explain, by telling my Reader, that tho' I have not said so in express Words yet I design therby to mean such Laymen, as either Act, 1st, in opposition to the Episcopal Authority, or else 2dly, not in Subordination to it.* " whether Bishops, the Spiritual Governours of the Church, " who have power from Christ to give a Man a standing Com- " mission to be a Priest, cannot give him a Commission *pro hac* " *vice,* in Cases of extream necessity, to do a Sacerdotal Act, *I will not presume to determine, neither do I think it necessary to dispute against those, who affirm that they can ; provided the Layman be in communion with, and an actual Member of that Particular National, or Provincial Church, over which the Bishops preside who give such an Occasional Commission, provided also, that they give him the Commission in such a manner, and with such Limitations and Restrictions, as that ther may be no more reason to suspect the Truth of* the Divine Authority residing in him for the executing of that Sacerdotal Act *pro hic & nunc,* in a Case of extream necessity, than ther is to question the Validity of the standing Commission of the ordinary Priesthood; *for then, in such Case, the Man also not of himself, or as a mere Laick ; he is suppos'd not to Administer, by vertue of any Canon of Foreign Councils, but as impower'd by the Authority of those particular Bishops he is subject to ; and I think it necessary to make these Provisoes, because on the other Hand it is well known, how apt Men have been, and still are, to pervert and abuse this Power and Authority, and misapply it to wrong and ill Purposes by unsound and false Inferences,* (as I my self have found by Experience in my Conversation, relating to my own particular Case) *so far as at last to make the Christian Priesthood be esteem'd by the heedless Multitude, as a thing of no necessary use and value at all, and for this Reason 'tis that I have endeavour'd so much (in this Essay Page* 83. *and Appendix Page* 155. *and* 156.) *to shew the ill uses which Men are apt to make of the Churches Power.*

After all, whether a Church has or has not the Power of Authorizing her own Laicks (as above specified) to Baptize in Cases of Extremity, I think I need make no scruple to say.

1st, *That the practice of one National or Provincial Church in this Case cannot Authorize the Laicks of another such Church, which gives them no such Authority.* —— (*as here with us.*)

2dly, *That no Church can have any Power to allow Laicks of opposite Communions to her, to administer Baptism in that Case, much less when ther is no necessity at all, (as certainly ther is none in our Dissenters Baptisms.)*

3dly, *That no Church has or can have power to confirm Baptisms so administered, because Confirmation supposes the Person to have been validly baptiz'd before, and his Baptism to be consummated and finish'd therby.*

A

THE
Author's Premonition
TO THE
READER.

THE occasion of writing this Essay is sufficiently declar'd in the Title Page; and the Design thereof is to contribute something towards the recovery of those, who are almost drowned in the fatal Error, of thinking that they receive Christian Sacraments, when in Truth and Reality they receive none at all. I don't doubt but I shall procure to my self many Enemies by this Attempt, but no matter for that, if this, my poor endeavour, can but prove effectual to stir up the Clergy (whose Office it is) to Preach and Write frequently, to disabuse Mankind in so weighty an Affair.

I am well aware, how diligent the Adversaries will be to find what Faults they can; and I am not so vain, as to think my self to have escaped altogether free from some in this Essay. And therfore, that I may take away all Occasions of unnecessary dispute, and save my self the trouble of future Answers to what may be cavil'd at by some, I shall here once for all declare what I think necessary, for the more clear Explanation of my Design and Meaning in some Passages of this Book, which otherwise I fear may give offence. And,

1st In the Preliminary Discourse

Page 13. I have noted from Du Pin, that "The Council of Ne-" ocœsarea, Anno 314, Canon I. says, that if a Priest marries " after he has been Ordain'd, he ought to be DEGRADED, whereas, in Truth that Author should have said, he ought to forbear the Exercise of his Office.

Page 20. I remark, that " the Hereticks and Schismaticks " were suppos'd to be EXCOMMUNICATE; my meaning is, that they were esteem'd AS EXCOMMUNICATE, because they separated from the Communion of the Church; and the same is meant of the known Excommunicated Hereticks and Schismaticks a little lower.

Page 23. My Censure of the Church may be reckon'd too harsh and severe for those early Days of Christianity; but I design no more
therby

To the READER.

therby than to represent that " *after Anno* 300 *she BEGAN to be,* (*not that she actually was immediately after that Period*) " *miserably* " over-run with Error and Superstition. *From that time ther was a gradual Declension from the Apostolick Purity ; and tho' the Faith was kept Whole and Entire, yet ther were some Mixtures made, some bad Foundations laid for after Miseries and Confusions, which infested more especially the Roman Church, to whom I had an Eye in that Censure. And I cannot see, but the Canons concerning the Celebacy of the Priests (tho' grounded on the general practice of the Primitive Clergy) gave occasion to the Church of Rome afterwards absolutely to forbid the Clergy Marriage, and to oblige them to vow Celebacy, as if Marriage were an Abomination to that Order of Men.*

Page 24. *I say,* " The Decrees of Fathers and Councils have " no more weight with me in this matter (*i. e. of Lay Baptism*) " than what they receive, from their Conformity to those Di- " vine Oracles, &c. *Here some may probably ask me,* " who must be judge between you and the Councils? *I answer, the same as must be judge between the contradictious Canons of different Councils ; the same as must be judge between me and a Council that commands me to worship Saints and Angels,* &c. *Now who this is upon Earth I cannot tell ; a living infallible Judge we have none ; and therfore I must look for a Rule or Guide,* 1. e. *the Holy Scripture, and if the Councils and I differ about the sense of this Rule, I must have recourse to the BEST and PUREST Ages of Christianity, and see what the Apostolick Fathers and the Councils next after them understood by that Rule in the controverted Point. After all I must be allow'd a judgment of discretion for my self, in conjunction with a just deference to the Canons of that particular Church, wherof I am, or ought to be a Member ; and by all these Methods I am brought to conclude for my self, that Lay Baptism by one in opposition to the Church can never be Good and Valid*

Page 30. *Where I say that* " I am not to be put off with the " Authority of any great Names, separate from Scripture and Rea- " son, *I desire to be understood of Reason in the Object, as Learned Men call all Mediums or Arguments of Proof, among which for the Authority of the Scriptures, and the sense of them in disputed Places, I unfeignedly declare, I look upon the consentient Doctrine and Practice of the Primitive Church, to be the best and strongest Proof.*

2dly, *In the Essay it self*

Page 82 *I speak of the Council of* Eliberis, *Anno* 305. *as if it esteem'd Lay Baptism in Cases of Extremity, to be* " in some measure " Invalid, till it was perfected, *or rather mended by Imposition* " of the Bishop's Hands. *See the same again Page* 109. *The reason why I do so is, because some (with whom I conferr'd upon this Sub-ject)*

great Author of our moſt holy Religion:
and may he, by the bleſſed influences of his
Spirit, ſtir up many **moꝛe of you** to *Cry
aloud and ſpare not, to lift up your Voices
like a Trumpet, to ſhew the People their Tranſ-
greſſion, and thoſe who ſtrive with the Prieſt
their Sin,* Iſa. 58. 1. Hoſ. 4. 4. and Rom.
2. 8. That they may learn to **know** and
ſubmit to thoſe who are over them, (*in the
Lord*) *and who watch for their Souls,* Heb.
13. 17. That they *may eſteem them* **very
highly** *in love for their* **Woꝛks** *ſake,*
1 Theſſ. 5. 13. Becauſe they are *th Miniſ-
ſters of Chriſt, and Stewards of the* **Myſteries** *of God,* 1 Cor. 4. 1. That ſo ine
People may effectually be enabled to *mark*
and *avoid* thoſe, who tho' they come to
*us in Sheeps Cloathing, and transform them-
ſelves into the* appearance of *Apoſtles of
Chriſt, and Miniſters of Righteouſneſs,* are
yet inwardly *but ravening Wolves, falſe
Apoſtles, deceitful Workers, and Miniſters
of Satan, in* St. *Paul*'s Language; for
they *cauſe Diviſions and Offences contrary
to the Doctrines which we have Learn'd,
nay,* contrary to the very *Principles, or
Foundations of the Doctrine of Chriſt, of
Baptiſms, and of Laying on of Hands,* and
therfore ſhould be *avoided,* that we may
keep the Unity of the Spirit in the Bond
. of

of Peace ; which that we may all learn to do, and by your confentient **conftant warnings** be preferv'd from the dreadful fin of *hating Sound Doctrine, and heaping to our felves Teachers* deftitute of the Divine Commiffion, who *ferve not our Lord Jefus Chrift, but their own Bellies,* may God of his Infinite Mercy grant, *through Jefus Chrift, to whom be Glory for Ever and Ever.* Amen.

F I N I S.

Lightning Source UK Ltd.
Milton Keynes UK
UKHW021857280620
365591UK00013BA/517